ORIENTAL
CROSS STITCH

LESLEY TEARE

D&C
David and Charles

A DAVID & CHARLES BOOK
Copyright © David & Charles Limited
2007

David & Charles is an F+W Publications
Inc. company
4700 East Galbraith Road
Cincinnati, OH 45236

First published in the UK in 2007

Text, charted designs and artworks
copyright © Lesley Teare 2007
Photographs copyright ©
David & Charles 2007

The author and publisher have made
every effort to ensure that all the
instructions in the book are accurate
and safe, and therefore cannot accept
liability for any resulting injury, damage
or loss to persons or property, however
it may arise.

Names of manufacturers, fabric
ranges and other products are
provided for the information of
readers, with no intention to
infringe copyright or trademarks.

A catalogue record for this book is
available from the British Library.

ISBN-13: 978-0-7153-2469-1 hardback
ISBN-10: 0-7153-2469-1 hardback

ISBN-13: 978-0-7153-2470-7 paperback
ISBN-10: 0-7153-2470-5 paperback

Printed in China
by SNP Leefung
for David & Charles
Brunel House   Newton Abbot   Devon

Executive Editor Cheryl Brown
Editor Jennifer Proverbs
Desk Editor Bethany Dymond
Art Editor Prudence Rogers
Senior Designer Tracey Woodward
Project Editor and Chart Preparation
   Lin Clements
Production Controller Ros Napper

Visit our website at
www.davidandcharles.co.uk

David & Charles books are available
from all good bookshops; alternatively
you can contact our Orderline on 0870
9908222 or write to us at FREEPOST
EX2 110, D&C Direct, Newton Abbot,
TQ12 4ZZ (no stamp required UK only);
US customers call 800-289-0963 and
Canadian customers call 800-840-5220.

*To my sons JM and JY for
their support and interest,
my love*

Contents

Introduction

This exquisite collection of over 30 cross stitch designs sets out to give you an insight into a unique style that we are privileged to enjoy, with ideas taken from the ancient art, culture, pottery, textiles and plants of the Far East.

This culture continues to fascinate us today and *Oriental Cross Stitch* offers a wealth of images of the Orient – distinctive images that will inspire experienced stitchers as well as those new to cross stitch. I have used some of these images to decorate a wide range of projects, including stunning pictures, stylish table linen, beautiful cushions and many small keepsake gifts and cards, each piece bringing a sense of Oriental harmony and love of nature into your home.

Many of the designs in this book were inspired by elegant pictures from Japanese art, porcelain and textiles, which I find particularly beautiful. In East Asian designs, aspirations and ideas can be expressed quite literally through motifs and colours, and they can certainly be appreciated aesthetically without knowledge of their symbolic intent. Textiles were created for use during all the rituals and ceremonies that mark the passages and transitions of life in the Far East – weddings, birthdays and seasonal festivities are all arrayed with auspicious patterns.

Patterns based on natural phenomena, such as mountains, waves, whirlpools and the moon, are often most recognizable as being distinctively Japanese. Plants too were a major design source and plant patterns came to Japan from China and India, as well as from Greece, Rome and Persia by way of tools, Buddhist articles, pieces of cloth and architectural items. As weaving, dyeing and painting techniques were developed all these patterns were refined and by the Edo period (1615–1868), a time of increasing prosperity and peace in Japan, they had achieved a high degree of brilliance.

This book captures some of the richness and diversity of Oriental culture, bringing you a collection of varied projects, all easy to stitch and make up. You will also find that the designs are highly versatile, and suggestions are made throughout for other ways to use the designs or smaller motifs from them.

Using colours and materials that evoke the sumptuous finish of Oriental dress and interiors, these elegant and exotic cross stitch designs will bring a touch of the Orient to your home.

These two companion designs of a brave samurai warrior and his sweetheart in her gorgeous kimono symbolize the essence of Oriental culture

4

Fan and Lantern

This attractive cross stitch design celebrates two key Oriental objects – the fan and the lantern. During the Lantern Festival, which originated in 230BC, the Chinese raise lanterns to catch a glimpse of deceased loved ones thought to be journeying to the heavens. Close proximity to neighbours is common in China and the placement of lanterns is not just for decoration but serves as a communication link in residential areas. A red lantern outside a doorway announces a birth or marriage, because red denotes vitality and energy. A blue lantern warns of sickness. White signifies death, so a white sash draped across the top of the doorway flanked by two white lanterns indicates that the family is in mourning.

In China there are four main types of fan: silk, folding, feather and palm. The silk fan is called the round fan because of its full-moon shape. The frame is usually made of iron or bamboo slips, with silk stretched over the frame, which is decorated with coloured images. This type of fan was popular with ladies in the royal court who came from wealthy families. Folded fans were introduced to China from Japan and Korea 1,000 years ago and the emperors and their ministers used this type of fan. They were usually made of fine paper mounted on bamboo and scholars often painted poetic and artistic expressions on the surface. The mounts or handles were of ivory, sandalwood or mottled bamboo and were carved with birds, flowers, landscapes and even poems.

This design has many motifs and is very versatile. Stitch it as a lovely picture or use motifs for smaller projects – see suggestions overleaf.

> *It retains coolness even in summertime and produces wind all year round. From your hand it brings autumn and under your arms it hides like a moon.*
>
> Description of a white-feather fan, Bai Juyi 8th century

Stitching the
Fan and Lantern Picture

This beautifully coloured design has been framed with a gold brocade fabric mount but a plain card mount could be used instead. Two charms are used in the design but you could stitch the areas if preferred. The many motifs within the design are perfect for small projects, such as the compact mirror shown right.

Stitch count 140h x 111w
Design size 25.5 x 20cm (10 x 8in)

You will need
- 36 x 31cm (14 x 12in) antique white 14-count Aida
- DMC stranded cotton (floss) as listed in the chart key
- Tapestry needle size 24 and a beading needle
- Kreinik #4 Very Fine Braid, 002 gold
- Mill Hill glass seed beads, 00557 gold and 02014 black
- Two charms (optional)
- 48 x 41cm (19 x 16in) background fabric for mount
- Black cord to trim embroidery
- Suitable picture frame

1 Prepare for work, referring to page 89 if necessary. Mark the centre of the fabric and centre of the chart overleaf. Mount your fabric in an embroidery frame if you wish.

2 Begin stitching from the centre of the fabric and work outwards. Work the full and three-quarter cross stitches using two strands of stranded cotton (floss) and one strand for Kreinik cross stitches. Work the backstitches using one strand.

3 Attach the beads where indicated on the chart, using a beading needle and matching thread (see page 91). If using charms do not stitch the diamond-shaped areas (shown by the blue dashed outlines on the chart) but attach the charms instead using matching thread.

4 Once all the stitching is complete attach it to the backing fabric if used (see page 94 for instructions) and finish your picture by mounting in a suitable frame (see page 93 for advice).

At this year's lantern festival
moonlight and lamplight shine no less
I have not seen my last year's love
tears wet the sleeves of my spring dress.

Ouyang Xiy (1007–1072)

Fan Compact Mirror

Stitch count 28h x 20w
Design size 5 x 3.6cm (2 x 1½in)

A handy compact mirror has been decorated with one of the smaller fan motifs from the main chart. Stitch the design on antique white 14-count Aida, using the main chart and key. Note: you will not need all of the colours. Follow the manufacturer's instructions for mounting the embroidery into the mirror case (see Suppliers).

Oriental Inspiration

- Make a case to hold the compact mirror using one of the lantern motifs. Attach the embroidery to a fabric case (see page 94) and edge the embroidery with decorative braid.

- The whole design would make a beautiful cover for a special photograph album or journal.

- You could stitch one of the vertical side panels on a smaller gauge fabric, such as a 16-count Aida or 32-count evenweave to make a charming bookmark.

- Use some of the smaller motifs in the design to decorate a collection of pretty trinket pots for a dressing table.

- The four corner designs would be perfect to adorn a set of square coasters.

- For a really quick project, stitch the outer pattern from the main chart on a length of Aida band for a simple bookmark, hemming the ends neatly.

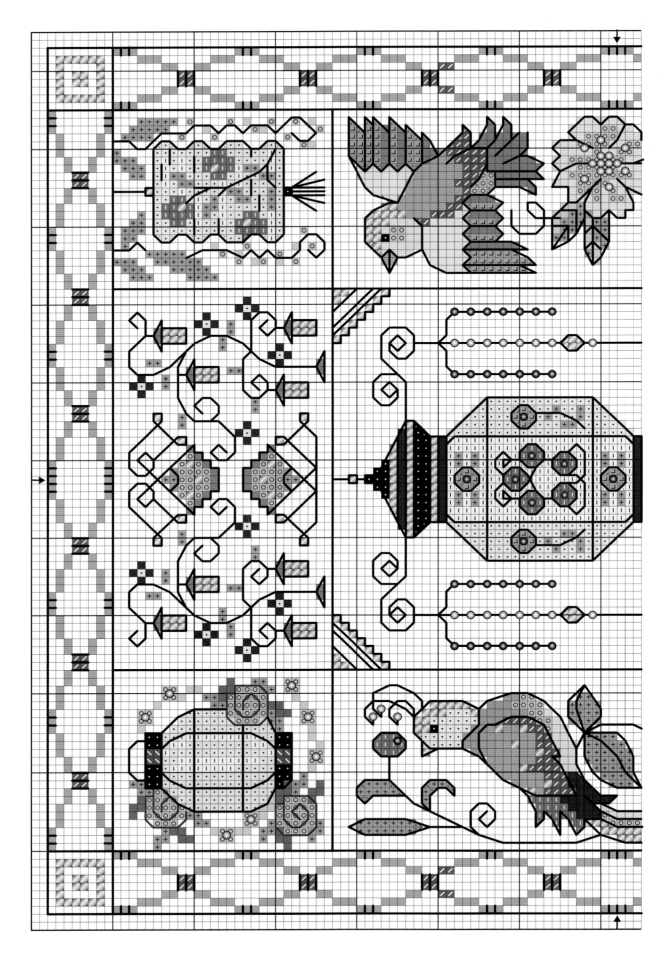

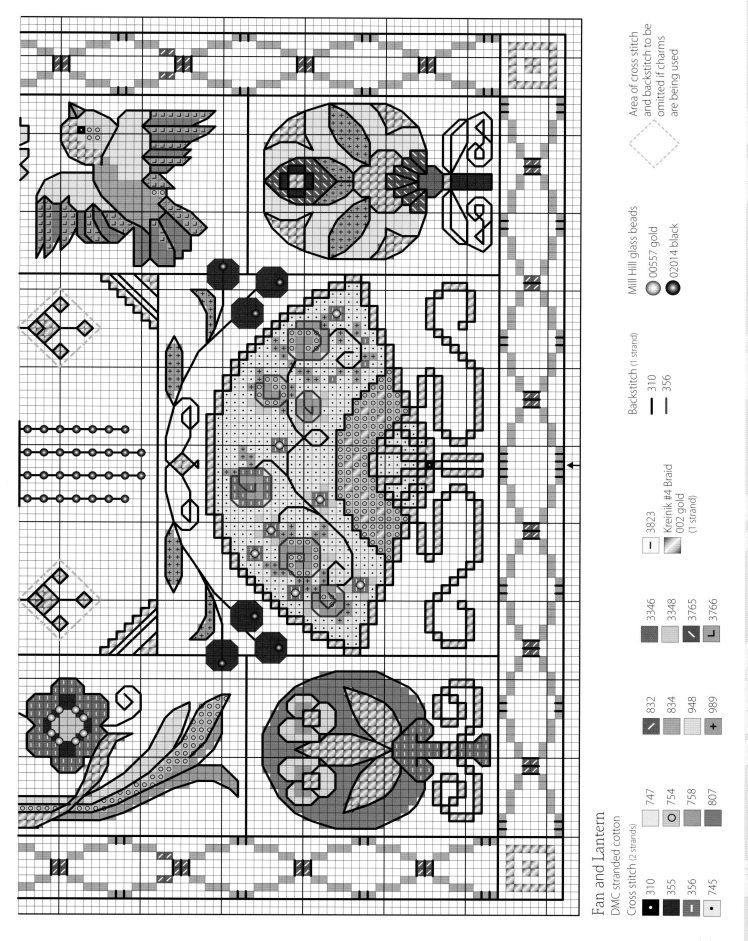

Area of cross stitch
and backstitch to be
omitted if charms
are being used

Mill Hill glass beads

○ 00557 gold
● 02014 black

Backstitch (1 strand)

── 310
── 356

I	3823
◪	Kreinik #4 Braid 002 gold (1 strand)

◪	3346		◪	832
◪	3348		◪	834
◪	3765			948
L	3766		+	989

Fan and Lantern
DMC stranded cotton

Cross stitch (2 strands)

●	310			747
◪	355		○	754
I	356			758
·	745		◪	807

Peacock and Peonies

This gorgeous design brings together two of the most beautiful icons in Oriental art. Peacocks and peonies are traditional symbols of wealth and prosperity in the Far East. Originally, peonies were costly and confined to the possession of the elite, so were quickly associated with wealth. If you could afford a peony in your garden you were indeed a rich family. The peony was one of the oldest plants cultivated for its flowers and the Chinese name for it is 'Sho Yo', meaning, most beautiful. The Chinese named the fourth month of their calendar as 'the moon of the peony', so when missionary Buddhist monks travelled to Japan, they took with them knowledge of the flower. The glorious pale pink peonies in the embroidery enhance the striking pose of the peacock, while soft foliage decorates the background.

The peony flowers having fallen we part without regret.
Tachibana Hokushi (1665–1718)

The Japanese first saw peacocks on Buddhist artwork from China. The bird is a symbol of beauty, reminding us to take pleasure in the finer things in life. The peacock is pure of heart, loyal and faithful to his partner. It is the male peacock that has beautiful iridescent blue-green plumage. His tail feathers have a series of eyes that are best seen when the tail is fanned. Here the stitched tail is elaborately rendered with the addition of gold and other metallic threads, which bring sparkle and iridescence to this beautiful cross stitch design.

This design looks wonderful displayed in a wooden needlework box, but it would look equally stunning made up in other ways – see overleaf for ideas. Two small motifs continue the theme, shown overleaf displayed in pot lids, one decorative and the other suitable to use as a pincushion.

Stitching the
Peacock and Peonies Box

This elegant design is shown on the previous page mounted into a wooden box lid but it would also make a fabulous framed picture or a sumptuous cushion.

Stitch count 121h x 148w
Design size 22 x 27cm (8¾ x 10½in)

You will need
- 43 x 51cm (17 x 20in) very pale pink 28-count linen (Brittney, Hint of Pink)
- Tapestry needle size 24
- DMC stranded cotton (floss) as listed in the chart key
- Kreinik #4 Very Fine Braid: 002V vintage gold, 006 blue and 085 peacock
- Wooden table-top workbox (see Suppliers)
- 25.5 x 30cm (10 x 11½in) wadding (batting)
- Double-sided adhesive tape
- Decorative braid
- Permanent fabric glue

1 Prepare for work, referring to page 89 if necessary. Mark the centre of the fabric and centre of the chart overleaf. Mount your fabric in an embroidery frame if you wish.

2 Begin stitching from the centre of the fabric and the centre of the chart and work outwards over two threads of the linen. Work the cross stitches using two strands of stranded cotton (floss) and one strand for the Kreinik cross stitches. Work all backstitches with one strand.

3 Once the stitching is complete, fit it into the lid of the workbox following the instructions on page 100 or the manufacturer's instructions. If you prefer you could make the design up as a cushion (see page 100 for instructions) or frame it as a picture (see page 93).

Trinket Pots

Trinket pot stitch count 27h x 31w
Design size 5 x 5.6cm (2 x 2¼in)

Pincushion stitch count 31h x 33w
Design size 5.6 x 6cm (2¼ x 2³/₈in)

This pretty trinket pot and pincushion feature one of the peony flowers and an 'eye' from the peacock's tail feathers. Stitch the designs on antique white 14-count Aida, following the charts and keys below, using two strands of stranded cotton for cross stitch and one strand for Kreinik cross stitches. Use one strand for backstitch. Mount the designs into the pot and pincushion according to the manufacturer's instructions (see Suppliers for sources).

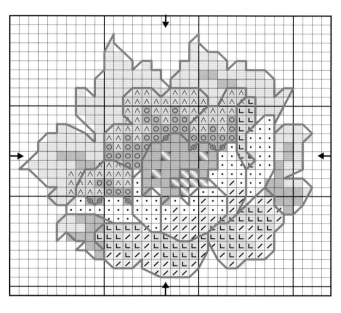

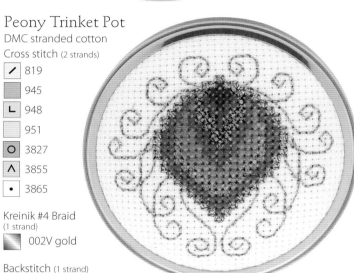

Peony Trinket Pot
DMC stranded cotton
Cross stitch (2 strands)

╱	819
▨	945
L	948
▨	951
O	3827
∧	3855
•	3865

Kreinik #4 Braid
(1 strand)

▨	002V gold

Backstitch (1 strand)

— Kreinik #4
002V gold

Peacock Eye Pincushion
DMC stranded cotton
Cross stitch (2 strands)

I	311
•	517
+	921
▨	3847
V	3853

Kreinik #4 Braid
(1 strand)

▨	002V gold
▨	006 blue
▨	085 peacock

Backstitch (1 strand)

— Kreinik #4
002V gold

Peacock and
Peonies
DMC stranded cotton
Cross stitch (2 strands)

■	310
I	311
■	434
•	517
╱	819
+	921
	945
L	948
	951
—	976
	977
╱	3808
	3814
O	3827
	3842
	3847
V	3853
∧	3855
•	3865

Kreinik #4 Braid
(1 strand)

	002V gold
	006 blue
	085 peacock

Backstitch (1 strand)
— 938
— Kreinik #4 Braid
002V gold

Geisha Triptych

*T*he idea for this triple design came from the beautiful posters of the Art Nouveau period, an era that was greatly influenced by Japan opening its frontiers to the West. I chose a narrow, vertical format to portray three geisha women, posed in decorated kimonos, each with their own flower. I have framed them together as a triptych but each would look beautiful framed alone so I have given individual instructions for the stitching of each design.

The Japanese character for 'gei' means 'of the arts' and 'sha' means 'person', so the word geisha literally means, a person of the arts. In fact, geishas were skilled performers in many traditional Japanese arts, including dance, music, flower arranging (*ikebana*), poetry, etiquette and conversation. Their precise way of dressing has become legend, particularly their kimonos.

*Early morning breeze
the scent of your silken hair
wakes me from slumber.*

Author unknown

The kimono was the common garment for Japanese woman as late as the 1940s. Today, Western dress is universal in Japan though the kimono is still worn on special occasions. The drape and cut of the garment has remained the same for decades, with variations only in pattern and colour. A rigid and complicated set of rules, as well as the unchanging factor of good taste, dictates the proper use of the kimono. Colours in traditional kimonos were chosen to reflect the season, occasion and social class. The fabrics became works of art and in the Edo period a woman's clothing was her principal form of property, with kimono collections becoming heirlooms.

Each of the geisha designs would look striking as a centrepiece for any room. Three pretty cards have also been created (page 23) using the geishas' signature flowers of peony, iris and chrysanthemum.

Stitching the Peony Geisha

This elegant geisha walks among peony flowers and the pretty blossoms also decorate her kimono and fan. A geisha's hair required combs and ornaments to keep elaborate styles in place and the way they were worn expressed fashionable elegance, position, distinction or special honour.

Stitch count 178h x 55w
Design size 32.3 x 10cm (12¾ x 4in)

You will need
- 51 x 23cm (21 x 9in) cream 14-count Aida
- Tapestry needle size 24
- DMC stranded cotton (floss) as listed in the chart key
- Suitable picture frame

1 Prepare for work referring to page 89 if necessary. Mark the centre of the fabric and centre of the chart (pages 24–25). Mount your fabric in an embroidery frame if you wish.

2 Begin stitching from the centre of your fabric and centre of the chart and work outwards. Work the full and three-quarter cross stitches using two strands of stranded cotton (floss). Work backstitches using one strand.

3 Once all the stitching is complete, finish your picture by mounting in a suitable frame (see page 93 for advice). I used a framing service to cut the triple mount and frame the triptych.

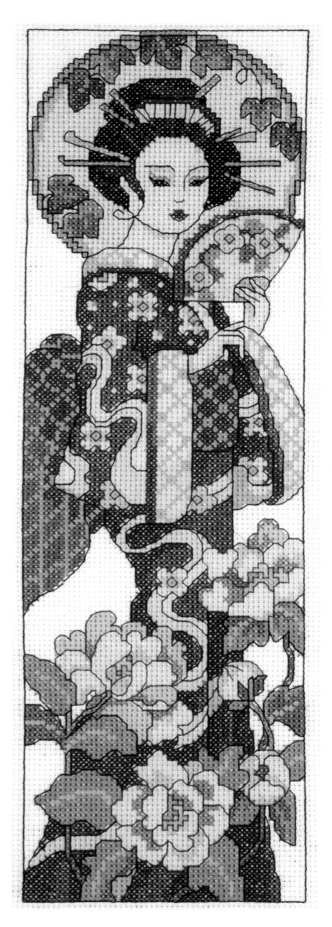

See page 23 for instructions on stitching this lovely peony card

Stitching the
Iris Geisha

This geisha wears a jacket or *haori* over her kimono, which means that she is attending a formal occasion. The colours of her kimono echo those of the iris flower.

Stitch count 178h x 55w
Design size 32.3 x 10cm (12¾ x 4in)

You will need
• 51 x 23cm (21 x 9in) cream 14-count Aida
• Tapestry needle size 24
• DMC stranded cotton (floss) as listed in the chart key
• Suitable picture frame

1 Prepare for work referring to page 89 if necessary. Mark the centre of the fabric and centre of the chart (pages 26–27). Mount your fabric in an embroidery frame if you wish.

2 Begin stitching from the centre of your fabric and centre of the chart and work outwards. Work the full and three-quarter cross stitches using two strands of stranded cotton (floss). Work backstitches using one strand.

3 Once all the stitching is complete, finish your picture by mounting in a suitable frame (see page 93 for advice). I used a framing service to cut the triple mount and frame the triptych.

Stitch this elegant iris card following the instructions on page 23

Stitching the Chrysanthemum Geisha

This pretty geisha stands among chrysanthemum flowers, the turning of the season also reflected in the tumbling maple leaves and autumnal colours of her kimono.

Stitch count 178h x 55w
Design size 32.3 x 10cm (12¾ x 4in)

You will need
- 51 x 23cm (21 x 9in) cream 14-count Aida
- Tapestry needle size 24
- DMC stranded cotton (floss) as listed in the chart key
- Suitable picture frame

1 Prepare for work referring to page 89 if necessary. Mark the centre of the fabric and centre of the chart (pages 28–29). Mount your fabric in an embroidery frame if you wish.

2 Begin stitching from the centre of your fabric and centre of the chart and work outwards. Work the full and three-quarter cross stitches using two strands of stranded cotton (floss). Work backstitches using one strand.

3 Once all the stitching is complete, finish your picture by mounting in a suitable frame (see page 93 for advice). I used a framing service to cut the triple mount and frame the triptych.

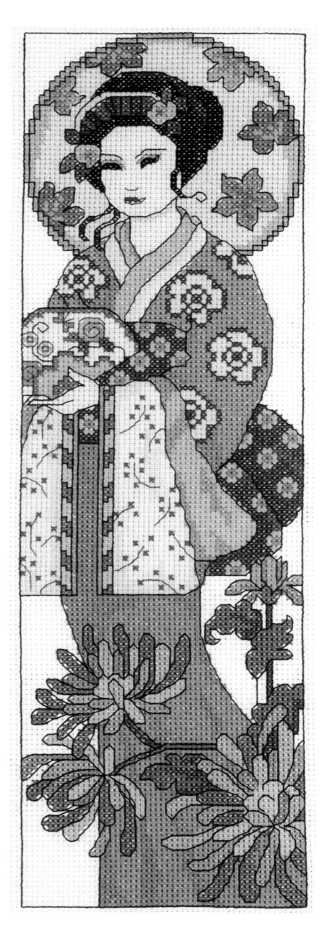

See opposite for instructions on stitching this striking chrysanthemum card

Stitching the Floral Cards

The three little flowers from the geisha designs have been stitched and mounted into arched cards, which creates a very pretty effect. You could work the flowers on a different colour Aida if desired. See the charts below for the stitch counts and design sizes.

You will need (for each card)
- 12.5 x 10cm (5 x 4in) white 14-count Aida
- Tapestry needle size 24
- DMC stranded cotton (floss) as in the chart key
- Double-sided adhesive tape
- Suitable card mount

1 Prepare for work, referring to page 89 if necessary. Mark the centre of the Aida and the centre of the chart.

2 Begin stitching from the centre of the chart and work outwards. Use two strands of stranded cotton (floss) for cross stitches and one strand for backstitches.

3 Once all stitching is complete, mount your embroidery in the card (see page 96).

Peony

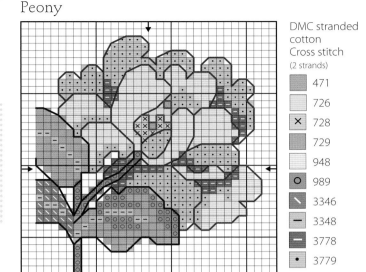

DMC stranded cotton
Cross stitch
(2 strands)
- 471
- 726
- × 728
- 729
- 948
- o 989
- \ 3346
- – 3348
- ▬ 3778
- • 3779

Backstitch
(1 strand)
— 869
— 919
— 3371

Stitch count 37 x 30
Design size 6.5 x 5.5cm (2¾ x 2⅛in)

Iris

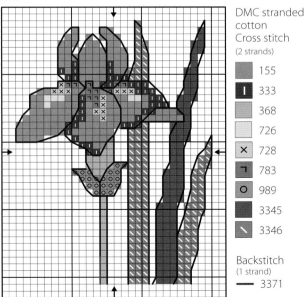

DMC stranded cotton
Cross stitch
(2 strands)
- 155
- I 333
- 368
- 726
- × 728
- ⌐ 783
- o 989
- 3345
- \ 3346

Backstitch
(1 strand)
— 3371

Stitch count 39 x 28
Design size 7 x 5cm (2¾ x 2in)

Chrysanthemum

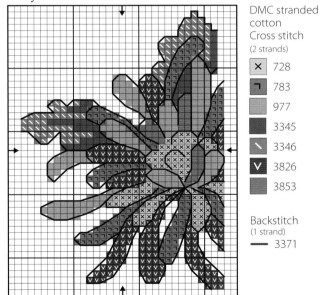

DMC stranded cotton
Cross stitch
(2 strands)
- × 728
- ⌐ 783
- 977
- 3345
- \ 3346
- v 3826
- 3853

Backstitch
(1 strand)
— 3371

Stitch count 44 x 31
Design size 8 x 5.5cm (3⅛ x 2¼in)

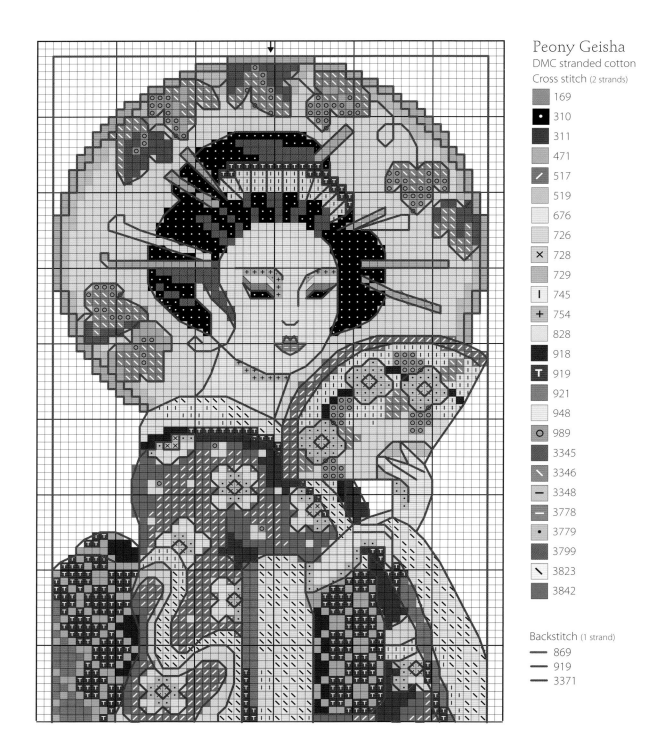

DMC stranded cotton
Cross stitch (2 strands)

	169
•	310
	311
	471
/	517
	519
	676
	726
×	728
	729
I	745
+	754
	828
	918
T	919
	921
	948
o	989
	3345
\	3346
–	3348
=	3778
•	3779
	3799
\	3823
	3842

Backstitch (1 strand)

—	869
—	919
—	3371

*The peony bud
when opening
shoots forth a rainbow.*

Yosa Buson (1716–83)

Iris Geisha

DMC stranded cotton
Cross stitch (2 strands)

	155
	169
⊙	310
I	333
	368
	726
✕	728
	729
I	745
+	754
˥	783
	797
L	798
	799
∧	800
	918
T	919
	948
	977
O	989
╲	3345
╲	3346
•	3779
	3799
╲	3823
V	3826

Backstitch (1 strand)

— 869
— 895
— 3371

This lone iris
white
in spring twilight.
Masaoka Shiki (1867–1902)

Chrysanthemum Geisha

DMC stranded cotton

Cross stitch (2 strands)

	169
•	310
✕	470
	471
	519
	676
✕	728
	729
I	745
+	754
﹁	783
	828
	918
T	919
	920
	948
	977
＼	3345
＼	3346
	3799
＼	3823
V	3826
	3853

Backstitch (1 strand)

——	869
——	895
——	3371

As I view chrysanthemums
my soul and heart are
gently enticed by the floral spirit.

Iida Dakotsu (1885–1962)

Oriental Landscapes

The pottery and porcelain of China was the inspiration for this charming picture. Pottery and porcelain has been produced in China longer than anywhere else and Dutch traders began importing it to Europe in the 17th century. No European maker had been able to produce such fine quality wares and there was a huge demand for it. Nearly all the porcelain was blue and white until around 1700 when more varied colours were introduced.

Chinese blue-and-white ceramics had long been admired and copied, and by the early 19th century English potters were producing large quantities of inexpensive transfer-printed earthenware to satisfy the growing market. The willow pattern design is one of the most famous British ceramic designs. Around 1790, Josiah Wedgwood was inspired by an original Chinese pattern called Mandarin. The design was based on a legend of a wealthy mandarin whose daughter fell in love with her father's secretary. To prevent an alliance she was imprisoned in the palace, but one day she escaped and the lovers raced over a bridge, chased by a servant, to a waiting boat. A storm developed, the boat foundered and the couple was lost at sea. It is said that two lovebirds appeared as their spirits.

I designed a group of three pictures to represent this story and framed them similarly to Chinese hanging scrolls. Instead of framing the designs, make them into a wall hanging by adding a backing fabric with a channel for a dowel rod or purchased bell pull. See overleaf for other suggestions.

Two birds flying high
a little ship passing by.
Weeping willow hanging o'er
bridge with three men, if not four.
Chinese temples there they stand
seem to take up all the land.
Apple trees with apples on
a pretty fence to end my song.

An old Staffordshire song,
based on the willow pattern story

Stitching the
Willow Pattern Picture

The elegant picture is created by stitching the three designs separately and then mounting them in the picture frame. You will need a frame approximately 66 x 23cm (26 x 9in) for this. Refer to page 94 for mounting instructions. Alternatively, the designs can be used separately, perhaps for a set of three smaller pictures or as cards, as the example here shows.

Stitch count (for each design) 82h x 54w
Design size (for each design) 15 x 10cm (6 x 4in)

You will need (for the complete picture)
• Three pieces 25.5 x 20cm (10 x 8in) white 14-count Aida
• Tapestry needle size 24
• DMC stranded cotton (floss) as listed in the chart keys
• 76 x 35.5cm (30 x 14in) piece of background fabric
• Iron-on interfacing, such as Vilene
• 2m (2yd) of red silk braid
• Three decorative buttons
• Suitable picture frame

1 Prepare for work, referring to page 89 if necessary. Mark the centre of each piece of fabric and the centre of each chart (pages 33–35). Mount each fabric piece in an embroidery frame if you wish.

2 Begin stitching from the centre of the fabric and centre of the chart and work outwards. Work the full and three-quarter cross stitches using two strands of stranded cotton (floss) and backstitches with one strand. Work French knots with two strands wound once around the needle.

3 Once all the stitching is complete, refer to page 94 for attaching the embroideries to a background fabric and also to page 93 for framing.

Oriental Inspiration

• Stitch the pictures individually and apply to a tea cosy, apron or oven glove for matching ideas for the kitchen (see page 94 for attaching embroidery to a background fabric).

• Take small motifs from the pictures, such as the boat, the birds and the bridge, to create a set of teatime coasters.

Bluebird Card

Stitch count 77h x 21w
Design size 14 x 3.8cm (5½ x 1½in)

This stylish card features two bird motifs and the symbol for good luck but you could use other parts of the willow pattern designs. These motifs are charted opposite and are stitched on white 14-count Aida, using two strands of thread for cross stitch and one for backstitch. The coin (available from larger craft stores) is also a good luck symbol in Oriental culture, and is added with narrow white ribbon as a decoration. See page 96 for mounting work in cards.

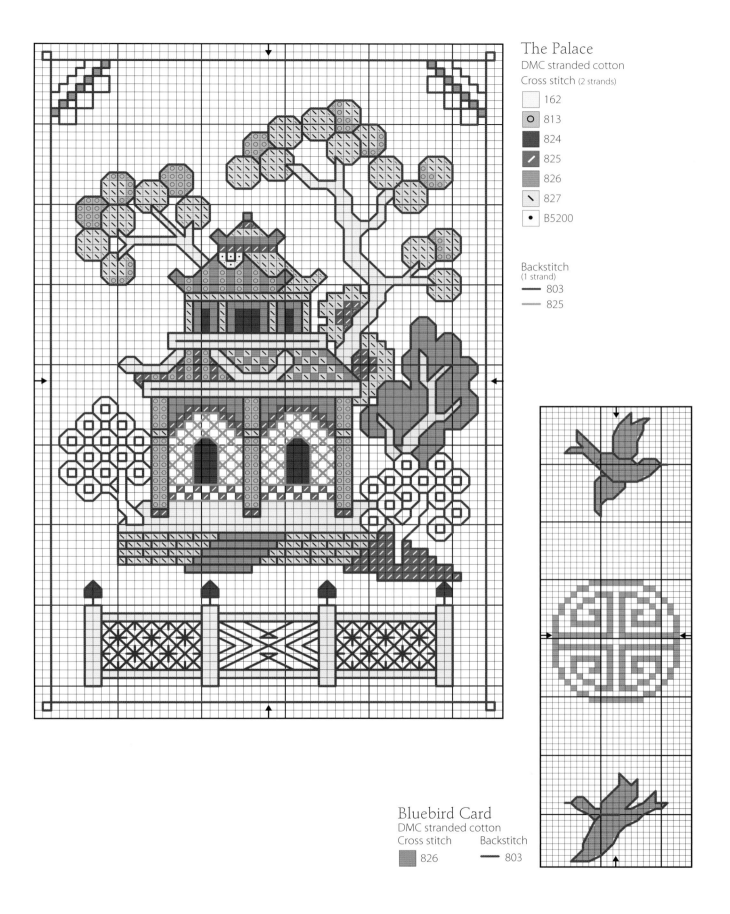

The Palace
DMC stranded cotton
Cross stitch (2 strands)

	162
O	813
	824
/	825
	826
\	827
•	B5200

Backstitch
(1 strand)
— 803
— 825

Bluebird Card
DMC stranded cotton

Cross stitch	Backstitch
826	— 803

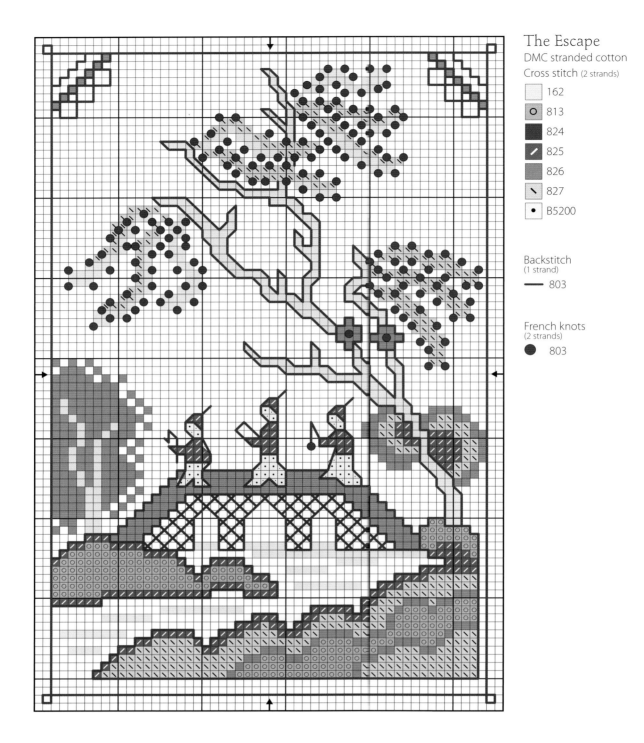

The Escape

DMC stranded cotton
Cross stitch (2 strands)

	162
○	813
■	824
╱	825
	826
╲	827
•	B5200

Backstitch
(1 strand)
—— 803

French knots
(2 strands)
● 803

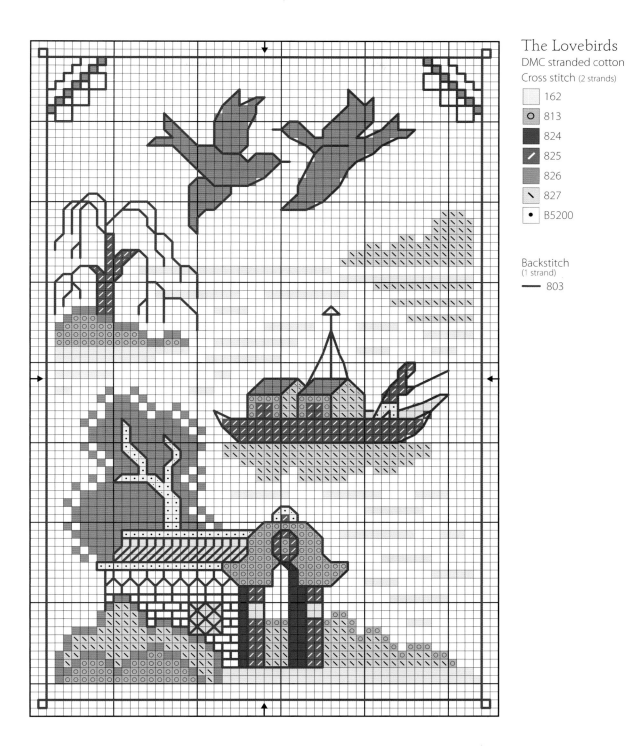

The Lovebirds
DMC stranded cotton
Cross stitch (2 strands)

☐	162
⊙	813
■	824
◪	825
◩	826
◫	827
•	B5200

Backstitch
(1 strand)
— 803

We were together
only a little while
and we believed our love
would last a thousand years.
Ohtomo Yakamochi (717–785)

Mandarin Ducks

For centuries in the Far East Mandarin ducks have been symbols of love, romance, devotion, fidelity, affection and partner loyalty. They have an ornate and distinctive plumage and I have used these attractive birds as the focal point on a sumptuous cushion design.

Mandarin ducks were originally from Asia, where the species was once widespread but they are now endangered because of destruction of forest habitat. In the wild, they breed in densely wooded areas near shallow ponds, lakes and marshes and nest in cavities in trees close to the water. A migratory bird in Asia, they overwinter in the lowlands of eastern China and southern Japan.

Evening snow falling
a pair of mandarin ducks
on an ancient lake.
Masaoka Shiki (1863–1913)

As with many of the Mandarin ducks to be found in Chinese art they present an idealized picture and my design is no exception. Due to the attractive shape of the birds, these patterns are often very beautiful. These two have a backdrop of rippling water stitched in gold thread, with autumn maple leaves floating down from the trees into the water. There is a famous *tatsutagawa* pattern of red maple leaves floating on water, named after the Tatsuta River in Nara Prefecture, in the centre of Japan, which is famed for this spectacle. This popular pattern of water and leaves has been used in textile patterns for many decades as well as portrayed on pottery and lacquer work.

Worked on a soft pink Juliana linen, I used metallic thread to pick out details of the birds' feathers, so that although the design is simple to stitch the end result is pretty and elegant, making it ideal for an attractive cushion.

Stitching the Duck Cushion

This design has the added sparkle of gold metallic thread and has been made up into a cushion, given a luxurious look by being embellished with golden tassels.

Stitch count 122h x 224w
Design size 22 x 41cm (8¾ x 16in)

You will need

- 56 x 41cm (22 x 16in) soft pink 28-count Zweigart Juliana linen
- Tapestry needle size 24
- DMC stranded cotton as listed in the chart key
- Kreinik #4 Very Fine Braid, 002 gold
- Backing fabric same size as trimmed embroidery
- Four tassels (optional)
- Decorative cord (optional)
- Cushion pad to fit

1 Prepare for work, referring to page 89 if necessary. Mark the centre of the fabric and centre of the three-part chart (pages 39–41). Mount your fabric in an embroidery frame if you wish.

2 Begin stitching from the centre of the fabric and centre of the chart and work outwards over two threads of the linen. Work the full and three-quarter cross stitches with two strands of stranded cotton (floss) and one strand for Kreinik cross stitches. Work the black backstitches with one strand.

3 Make the design up into a cushion following the instructions on page 100. Check the size of the cushion pad needed, as you may need to add more gold cross stitches to take the line out to the edges of the cushion. You could add decorative cord around the edge of the finished cushion if desired, or make a simple twisted cord as an edging (see page 102 for instructions).

Oriental Inspiration

- The design would make an impressive picture, especially if double mounted within an ornate gold frame.

- Why not work the two ducks individually as two small, circular pillows?

- The three whole maple leaves could be worked individually on linen to make a set of coasters. Fray the edges of the linen for a pretty finishing touch.

*Water birds going and coming
their traces disappear
but they never forget their path.*
Eihei Doogen (1200–53)

Mandarin Ducks

DMC stranded cotton

Cross stitch (2 strands)

•	310
	677
	747
∧	807
	830
O	831
	975
—	976
	977
	3045
T	3046
L	3765
L	3766
/	3808
	3826
V	3827
+	3855
\	ecru
•	blanc
	Kreinik #4 Braid 002 gold (1 strand)

Backstitch (1 strand)

— 310

Mandarin Ducks
DMC stranded cotton
Cross stitch (2 strands)

⊡	310
	677
	747
∧	807
▨	830
⊙	831
▨	975
−	976
▨	977
▨	3045
T	3046
▨	3765
L	3766
▱	3808
▨	3826
V	3827
+	3855
⟍	ecru
•	blanc
▨	Kreinik #4 Braid 002 gold (1 strand)

Backstitch (1 strand)
— 310

Samurai Warrior

This splendid samurai warrior is a companion piece to the lovely Oriental Beauty design on page 76. The design makes an impressive picture as the warrior, in full samurai dress, gazes into the distance, pining for his love so far away.

The samurai tradition is unique to Japanese history. The word 'samurai' originally meant 'those who serve in close attendance to nobility'. As the venerated guardian of the people, the samurai were trained from birth to respect birthright and to attain the highest honours

Will you turn toward me?
I am lonely too,
this autumn evening
Matsuo Basho (1644–94)

of their class. This class was next to the Imperial family in the strict social strata of Japanese society. The samurai class had the means to fund many arts and many of Japan's fine arts and crafts are based on samurai culture.

The basic clothing item in a samurai's everyday wardrobe was the kimono, which for men consisted of an outer and inner layer. Between the 12th and 17th centuries the *hitatare* style of dress, a two-piece costume, was popular, usually adorned with the family crest. Footwear was mainly sandals (*wataji*) and wooden clogs (*geta*). The samurai's hair was an important part of his appearance and was traditionally worn as a topknot. His long sword was thrust through a belt (*obi*), worn wrapped around the waist and tied in front, while a short sword (*wakazashi*) was worn through the *obi*. The sword was worn on the left side, and although it was originally a highly practical item, in time it became more of a fashion statement.

A wild goose is included in this design as they are considered bearers of happiness and, in this picture, hope. This links in with the Oriental Beauty picture, which shows the samurai's sweetheart waiting for his return, accompanied by a butterfly to represent luck and protection.

Stitching the Samurai Picture

This impressive warrior would look wonderful in a study, either alone or paired with the Oriental Beauty design.

Stitch count 207h x 77w
Design size 37.5 x 14cm (14¾ x 5½in)

You will need

- 53 x 30.5cm (21 x 12in) antique white 14-count Aida
- Tapestry needle size 24
- DMC stranded cotton (floss) as listed in the chart key
- Kreinik #4 Very Fine Braid, 002 gold
- Suitable picture frame

1 Prepare for work, referring to page 89 if necessary. Mark the centre of the fabric and the three-part chart (pages 45–47). Mount your fabric in an embroidery frame if you wish.

2 Begin stitching from the centre of the fabric and centre of the chart and work outwards. Work the full and three-quarter cross stitches using two strands of stranded cotton (floss). Work the Kreinik gold cross stitches with one strand. Work all backstitches using one strand of thread.

3 Once the stitching is complete, finish your picture by mounting in a suitable frame (see page 93 for advice).

> *On Kasuga plain*
> *between those patches of snow*
> *just beginning to sprout,*
> *glimsped, the blades of grass,*
> *like those glimpses of you.*

Mibu no Tadamine (10th century poet)

Samurai Warrior

DMC stranded cotton
Cross stitch (2 strands)

⌐	729
╱	745
•	746
	762
▬	777
■	814
	869
⟨	3350
╱	3799
╱	3807
∣	3829
◲	Kreinik #4 Braid 002 gold (1 strand)

■	150
○	152
	156
	158
	223
╱	224
	225
•	310
	327
	550
╱	552
	676

Backstitch (1 strand)

———	310
———	223
———	535
———	Kreinik #4 Braid 002 gold

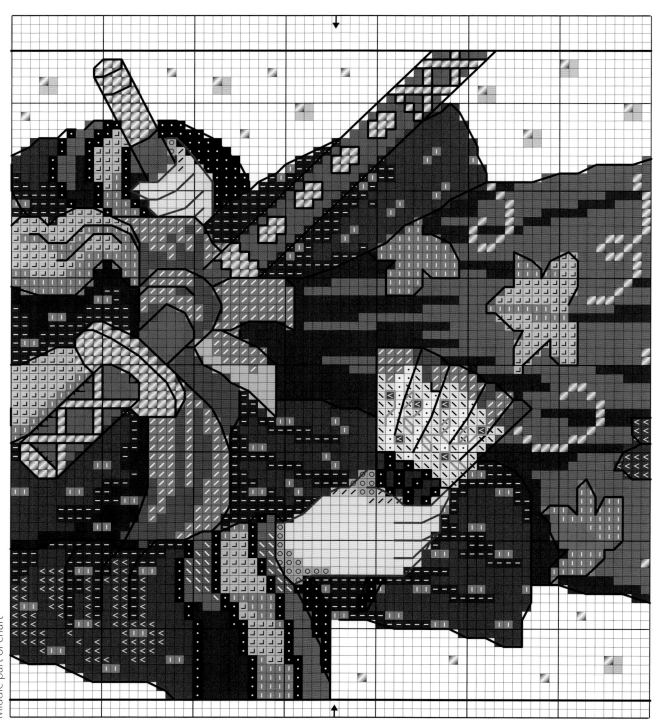

Middle part of chart

⌐ 729	150	
╲ 745	○ 152	
· 746	156	
762	158	
▬ 777	223	
■ 814	╱ 224	
869	225	
⋀ 3350	▪ 310	
3799	327	
╱ 3807	550	
▬ 3829	╱ 552	
◪ Kreinik #4 Braid 002 gold (1 strand)	676	

Backstitch (1 strand)

— 310
⸻ 223
⸻ 535
⸻ Kreinik #4 Braid 002 gold

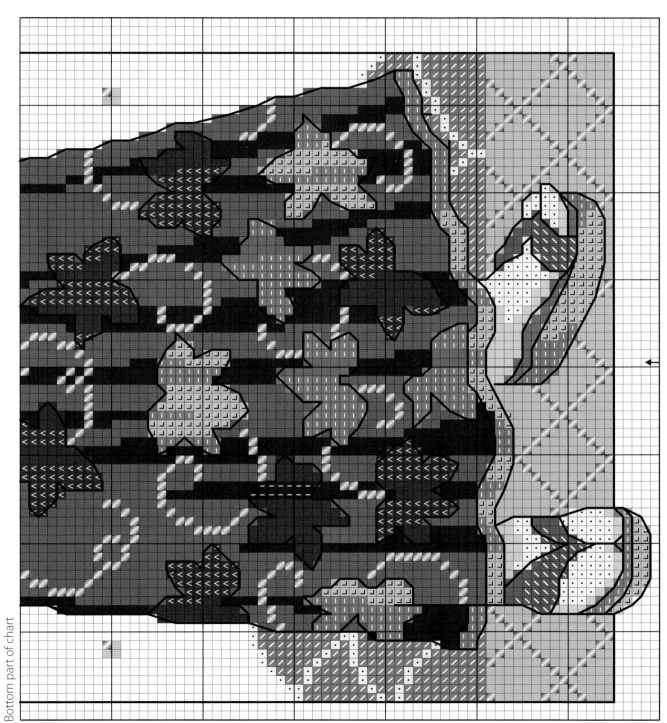

Bottom part of chart

Oriental Blooms

The Japanese have a deep respect for all growing things and in their culture certain flowers have special meanings, for example, the magnolia represents tenderness and love of nature. Drawings and paintings of flowers are used extensively to decorate clothing, furniture and even family crests. Many Japanese homes have an alcove or special place that is decorated with flowers and plants to show the changing of the seasons, and a home is considered very lucky if it has a plant that blooms on New Year's Day, for this foretells a year of prosperity. Some flowers, such as the peony, are believed to be symbolic of wealth and high position in one's career. Flowers and flower-giving are not seen as exclusively for women; Samurai warriors treasured flowers, particularly cherry blossom, taking the short-lived blooms as an expression of their way of life.

In joy or sadness, flowers are our constant friends.

Kozuko Okakura (1863–1913)

To celebrate the beautiful flowers of the Orient, I have designed a collection of floral motifs featuring nine of the best-loved flowers – the peony, morning glory, orchid, bellflower, poppy, magnolia, camellia, hydrangea and iris. In the picture opposite you will see how they have been worked together to create a beautiful framed picture. However, if you are running short of time, you can stitch the flowers individually to decorate a pretty bag and a charming coin purse (shown overleaf), or perhaps a pretty cushion. The designs are very versatile and would also be ideal for many other keepsake gifts and greetings cards. See overleaf for all stitching instructions.

Stitching the Individual Flowers

The flowers can be stitched individually to decorate many items, such as a bag and coin purse shown below. You could also use them on trinket pot lids, in coasters, sachets and cards for many occasions.

Stitch count (for each flower) 42h x 42w maximum
Design size 7.6 x 7.6cm (3 x 3in)

You will need (for each flower)
- 15 x 15cm (6 x 6in) white 14-count Aida
- Tapestry needle size 24
- DMC stranded cotton (floss) as listed in the chart key

1 Prepare for work, referring to page 89 if necessary. Mark the centre of the fabric and centre of the charted motif. Mount your fabric in a hoop or frame if you wish.

2 Begin stitching from the centre of the fabric and centre of the charted motif (pages 51–55), working outwards. Work all cross stitches using two strands of stranded cotton (floss) and backstitches with one strand. Work any French knots with two strands of thread.

3 When all the embroidery is completed, the work can be mounted in a card, framed as a small picture or made up into gifts. See page 99 for making up as a bag and page 101 for making a purse.

Stitching the Grouped Flowers

If you would like to work the flowers grouped together for a picture or a cushion, either stitch the group as shown in the plan below or arrange the flowers into your own composition. For your own use, you could photocopy the charts and place them into a pleasing arrangement.

Stitch count (for all flowers together) 154h x 154w
Design size 28 x 28cm (11 x 11in)

You will need

- 51 x 51cm (20 x 20in) white 14-count Aida
- Tapestry needle size 24
- DMC stranded cotton (floss) as listed in the chart key
- Suitable mount and picture frame

1 Prepare for work, referring to page 89 if necessary. Mark the centre of the fabric and mount your fabric in an embroidery frame if you wish. For the picture, shown on page 49, I allowed 14 squares between each flower (see the plan below).

2 Begin stitching from the centre of the fabric and the centre of the poppy chart overleaf, working outwards. Work all cross stitches using two strands of stranded cotton (floss) and backstitches with one strand. Work any French knots with two strands.

3 When the embroidery is finished, display the design as desired. If making up as a framed picture, ask your framer to cut a mount with nine apertures cut to size to take the individual flowers. Choose a moulding to complement the stitched piece.
If making up as a cushion you could work backstitch in gold or a matching thread around each design. This backstitch will be 42 stitches wide and 42 stitches high and is shown as a brown line on the plan.

The **hydrangea** dates back thousands of years in Japanese horticultural history. It is valued for its seven colour changes during its life cycle, with flowers that are brilliantly coloured in the gloomy rainy season. Buddhists believe that the variety of colours reflects the transience of life.

Hydrangea

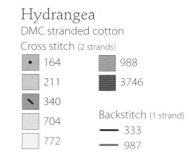

DMC stranded cotton
Cross stitch (2 strands)

•	164		988
	211		3746
\	340		
	704		Backstitch (1 strand)
	772	——	333
		——	987

Plan for stitching all flowers together
(measurements in Aida squares)

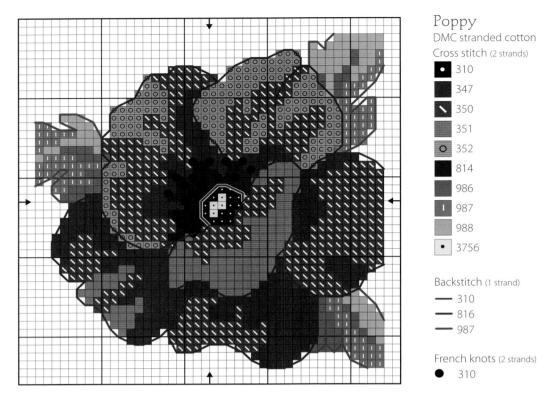

Poppy

DMC stranded cotton

Cross stitch (2 strands)

▣	310
■	347
◩	350
▨	351
◉	352
■	814
▨	986
▮	987
▨	988
▣	3756

Backstitch (1 strand)

— 310
— 816
— 987

French knots (2 strands)

● 310

The poppy is a vibrant and much-loved flower from Asia and means plant of joy. Only a handful of common garden flowers are to be found in medicine but the poppy is one of the most important. Morphine and codeine are two familiar analgesics made from this flower.

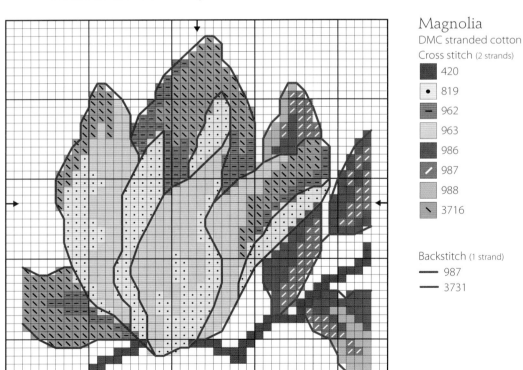

Magnolia

DMC stranded cotton

Cross stitch (2 strands)

■	420
▣	819
▤	962
▧	963
■	986
◪	987
▨	988
◩	3716

Backstitch (1 strand)

— 987
— 3731

The magnolia is a magical and mystical aristocrat that bursts into flower each spring and represents tenderness and love of nature. In Asia the magnolia was used in local herbal medicine because of its aromatic, stimulating and strengthening qualities.

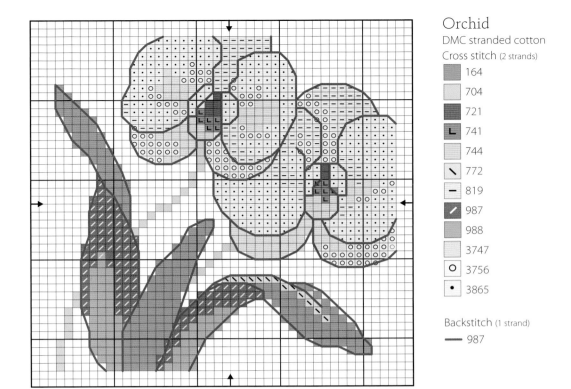

Orchid

DMC stranded cotton

Cross stitch (2 strands)

▨	164
▨	704
▨	721
L	741
▨	744
\	772
–	819
◪	987
▨	988
▨	3747
O	3756
•	3865

Backstitch (1 strand)

—— 987

The orchid is subtle and fragrant and is one of the four 'noble' plants in China, the others being plum blossom, chrysanthemum and bamboo. The orchid is a refined and elegant flower, a symbol of perfection, which brings a universal message of love, wisdom and thoughtfulness.

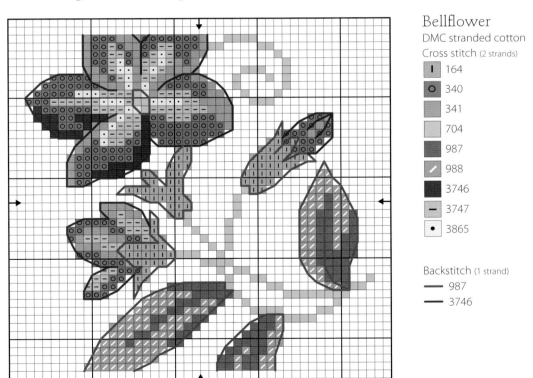

Bellflower

DMC stranded cotton

Cross stitch (2 strands)

I	164
O	340
▨	341
▨	704
▨	987
◪	988
▨	3746
–	3747
•	3865

Backstitch (1 strand)

—— 987
—— 3746

The bellflower is native to Western China and Tibet and is an exotic beauty that flowers from mid July to late August. It grows in grassy mountain highlands with temperate climates where its trumpet-shaped flowers, normally pink or purple, bloom in profuse clusters.

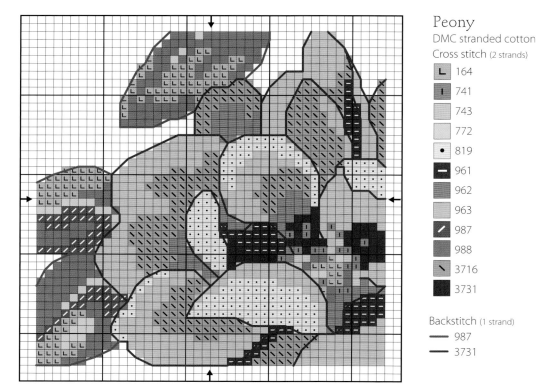

Peony

DMC stranded cotton

Cross stitch (2 strands)

L	164
I	741
	743
	772
•	819
▬	961
	962
	963
╱	987
	988
╲	3716
	3731

Backstitch (1 strand)

— 987

— 3731

The peony is the flower of June in Japan and a symbol of prosperity. For the Chinese, the peony symbolizes nobility and was the flower of their Empress. The lovely many-petalled blossom was often depicted on the houses, clothing and personal effects of the nobility.

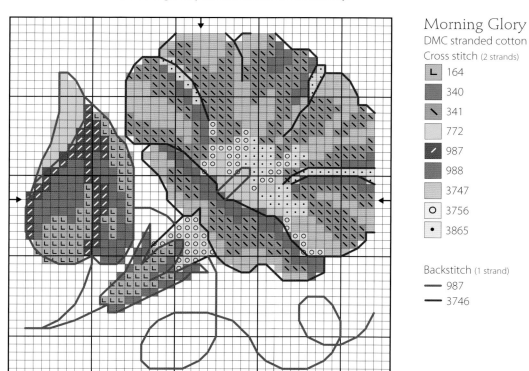

Morning Glory

DMC stranded cotton

Cross stitch (2 strands)

L	164
	340
╲	341
	772
╱	987
	988
	3747
O	3756
•	3865

Backstitch (1 strand)

— 987

— 3746

The morning glory was brought from China to Japan to be used for medical purposes and in Japan it became known as 'morning face' because it blooms in the morning, with the blossoms closing up very quickly. Its beauty, although brief, is a joy to be remembered.

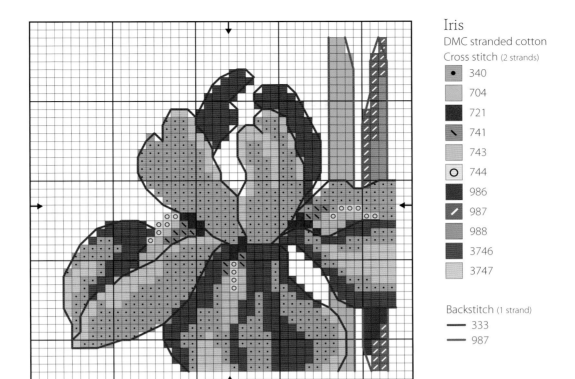

Iris
DMC stranded cotton
Cross stitch (2 strands)

- • 340
- 704
- 721
- ＼ 741
- 743
- ○ 744
- 986
- ╱ 987
- 988
- 3746
- 3747

Backstitch (1 strand)
— 333
— 987

The iris is a traditional flower loved by the Japanese and a symbol for faith, valour and wisdom. It was originally a symbol for Boys' Day – a festival in Japan that celebrated the hopes that young boys would grow up to be strong, wise and full of fighting spirit.

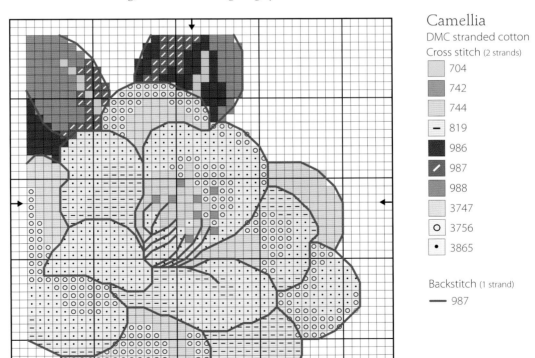

Camellia
DMC stranded cotton
Cross stitch (2 strands)

- 704
- 742
- 744
- — 819
- 986
- ╱ 987
- 988
- 3747
- ○ 3756
- • 3865

Backstitch (1 strand)
— 987

The camellia is considered to be a noble flower in the Far East and a symbol for prosperity. It is used in patterns for its showiness and variety of forms. All traditional Chinese tea is made from *Camellia sinensis*: different drying and processing produces the different varieties of green, black and oolong tea.

Crane Wedding

*T*his gorgeous wedding album uses the elegant crane as inspiration. Oriental legend holds that the crane lives for 1,000 years and in Japanese, Chinese and Korean tradition the bird represents peace and long life. Throughout Asia it is the symbol for peace, happiness, purity and fidelity and its image is used for happy occasions such as weddings and births. The motifs are used in Japanese weddings, wedding kimonos and decorations, for cranes mate for life and are devoted to their partners.

The album uses a linen band as this is a quick and effective way to personalize a ready-made album but the design could also be stitched on Aida fabric. The flowing lines of the birds are created within the shape of their bodies and elongated legs, while the detailed formation of the wings and tail feathers create a linear quality that is ideal for this design. Gold thread was used to highlight the embroidery, adding an attractive sparkle to the birds.

To what shall I liken the world? Moonlight, reflected in dewdrops shaken from a crane's bill.

Eihei Doogem (1200–53)

Red is an auspicious colour in the Far East, associated with warmth and denoting good fortune, so I used red to stitch a simple backstitch design around the cranes and the Chinese symbol, which means double happiness. In China, the colour red not only serves to express joy but also to ward off evil influences and so it is regarded as a lucky colour. It features prominently in wedding clothing and traditional ceremonies – Chinese brides wear red dresses and wedding invitations are printed on red paper.

The design for the ring cushion echoes the gold and red theme of the album. Worked on white linen, the cushion is simple to make up and is beautifully finished off by a white tassel and a red heart-shaped bead.

Stitching the Wedding Album

This beautiful album (shown on the previous page) is very quick and simple to stitch as it is mostly backstitch. The red and gold colouring is very striking and typically Oriental but you could change the colours if desired – try royal blue and silver for a different look.

Stitch count 120h x 62w
Design size 22 x 11.25cm (8½ x 4½in)

You will need

- 15.3cm (6in) wide 28-count natural linen band with ivory chevron edge, double the length of your album
- Tapestry needle size 24
- DMC stranded cotton (floss) as listed in the chart key
- Kreinik #4 Very Fine Braid, 003 red and 028 citron
- Iron-on interfacing the length and width of the linen band
- Photograph album
- Double-sided adhesive tape
- Bead and tassel if required

1 Prepare for work, referring to page 89 if necessary. Mark the centre of the linen band and the centre of the chart overleaf. Mount your fabric in an embroidery frame if you wish.

2 Begin by stitching from the centre of your band and centre of the chart and work outwards. Work the full and three-quarter cross stitches and the backstitches with one strand of stranded cotton or Kreinik thread. Work the French knots with one strand wound twice round the needle.

3 Once all the stitching is complete, attach the band to your album following the instructions on page 101.

*A watching crane
whoops far and wide
as the dawn approaches.*

Miura Yuzuru (dates unknown)

Oriental Inspiration

- Decorate some luxurious snowy-white bath towels by working the wedding album crane repeatedly along a length of 7.6cm (3in) wide Aida band. Slipstitch the band on to the towel turning the ends under neatly.

- Use the central motif to embellish a little gift bag for a bridesmaid. Either attach the motif as a patch on to a ready-made bag using iron-on interfacing or work the design on a larger piece of white or cream evenweave and make up as a bag, as described on page 99.

Stitching the Ring Cushion

This simple yet elegant wedding ring cusion is further enhanced by the addition of a white tassel and a gorgeous carved red bead in the shape of a heart.

Stitch count 66h x 135w
Design size 12 x 24.5cm (4¾ x 9¾in)

You will need

• 23 x 33cm (9 x 13in) antique white 28-count linen
• Tapestry needle size 24
• DMC stranded cotton (floss) as listed in the chart key
• Kreinik #4 Very Fine Braid, 028 citron and 003 red
• 23 x 33cm (9 x 13in) backing fabric
• Cushion pad
• Bead and tassel (optional)

1 Prepare for work, referring to page 89 if necessary. Mark the centre of the linen fabric and the centre of the chart on page 61. Mount your fabric in an embroidery frame if you wish.

2 Begin stitching from the centre of the fabric and centre of the chart and work outwards. Work the full and three-quarter cross stitches and backstitches with one strand of stranded cotton (floss) or Kreinik thread. Work the French knots with one strand wound twice round the needle.

3 Once all stitching is complete, trim the embroidery to the required size and make up into a cushion following the instructions on page 100. See page 102 for making your own tassel. If desired, you could add an edging of decorative braid or your own twisted cord – see page 102.

Good Luck Card

Stitch count 23h x 23w
Design size 4.2 x 4.2cm (1¾ x 1¾in)

This stylish card shows the symbol for good luck and is surrounded by a simple filigree in red backstitches. Follow the chart on page 61 and stitch the design on antique white 14-count Aida, using one strand of thread for cross stitches and backstitches. The addition of the coin (available from larger craft stores), also a symbol for good luck, is secured with a narrow gold ribbon and adds a personal touch to the card. See page 96 for mounting work in cards.

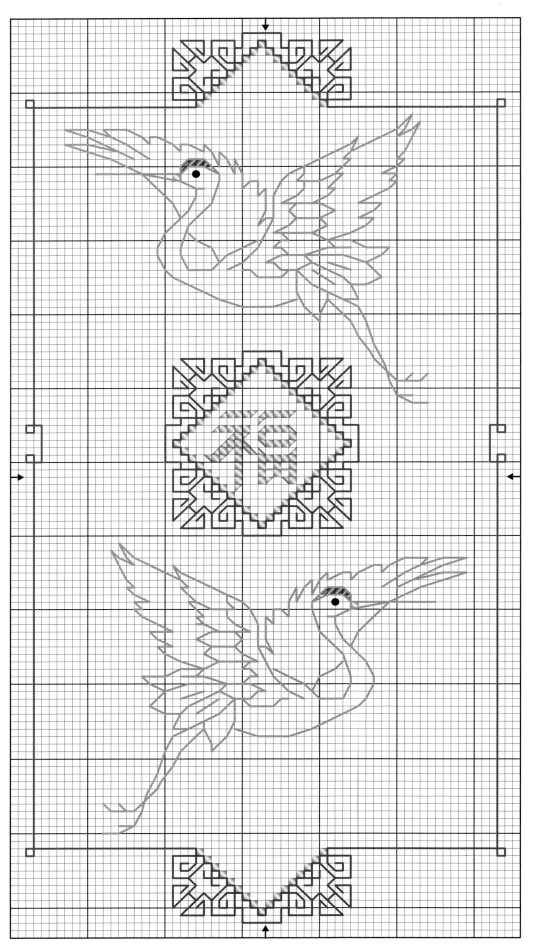

DMC stranded cotton
Cross stitch (1 strand)

 Kreinik #4 Braid
003 red

Kreinik #4 Braid
028 citron

Backstitch (1 strand)

— DMC 350

— Kreinik #4 Braid
028 citron

French knots (1 strand)

● 310

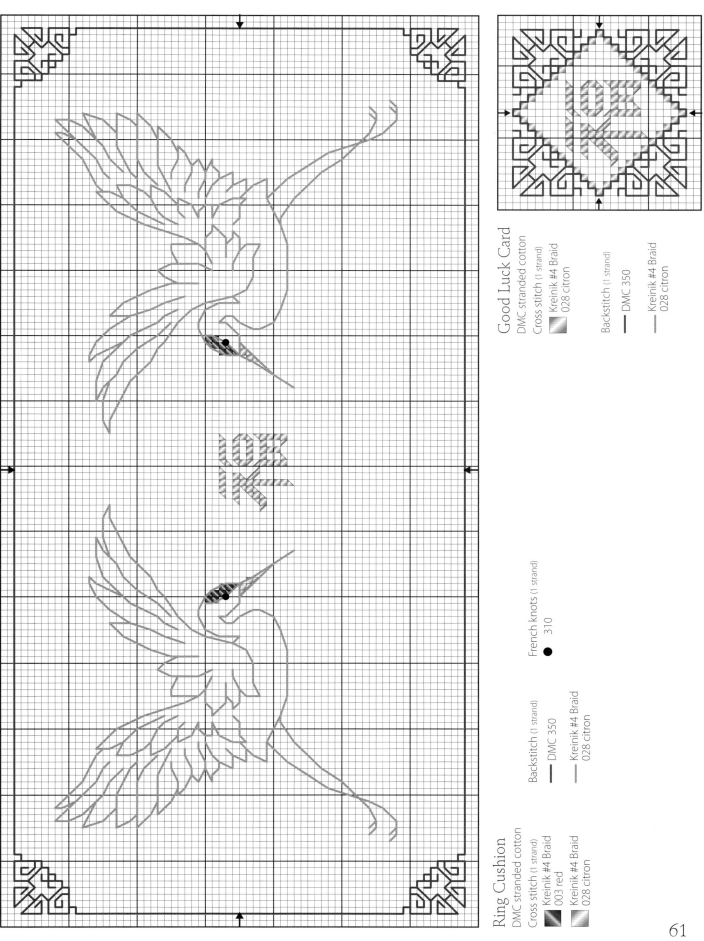

Good Luck Card

DMC stranded cotton

Cross stitch (1 strand)

▨ Kreinik #4 Braid
028 citron

Backstitch (1 strand)

— DMC 350

═══ Kreinik #4 Braid
028 citron

French knots (1 strand)

● 310

Backstitch (1 strand)

— DMC 350

═══ Kreinik #4 Braid
028 citron

Ring Cushion

DMC stranded cotton

Cross stitch (1 strand)

▨ Kreinik #4 Braid
003 red

▨ Kreinik #4 Braid
028 citron

Pagoda Splendour

The pagoda is a beautiful and distinctive style of building seen throughout the Far East, usually multi-storied with upwardly curving roofs. The style of pagoda I have used for this cross stitch picture is based loosely on Japanese temples. These tall structures usually have a balanced pyramidal shape, as well as exquisite decorative qualities. They are normally divided into five sections, corresponding to the five elements of earth, water, fire, wind and space. It is said that many facets of Japanese culture are depicted within a pagoda shape. My pagoda is also divided into sections, each one featuring different motifs and patterns. There are plant patterns that are both ornamental and structural and also birds, fishes and insects that are not only beautiful but considered auspicious, such as the dragonfly. This creature was considered a symbol of victory, which was why samurai warriors wore it on their armour.

With the cherry blossom gone the temple is glimpsed through twigs and branches.

Yosa Buson (1716–84)

The design as a whole makes a striking picture that would look stylish in any room, especially if set in a simple black frame and with the addition of some tassels. If you prefer, you can stitch smaller parts of the design: these sections are ideally shaped for working on Aida or linen bands and are perfect for creating a wide range of projects in next to no time. Using the gold borders as a guide, stitch the sections individually to create a pretty bag, a sweet little bracelet or a smart notebook – see overleaf for more suggestions and pages 93–101 for making up ideas.

Stitching the
Pagoda Picture

Nothing is more evocative of the Orient than the distinctive architecture, as this splendid pagoda design shows.

Stitch count 217h x 108w
Design size 39.5 x 19.5cm (15½ x 7¾in)

You will need
- 68 x 46cm (27 x 18in) antique white 14-count Aida
- Tapestry needle size 24 and a beading needle
- DMC stranded cottons (floss) as listed in the chart key
- Kreinik #4 Very Fine Braid, 202HL Aztec gold
- Mill Hill glass seed beads, 02014 black
- Four ready-made black tassels

1 Prepare for work, referring to page 89 if necessary. Mark the centre of the fabric and centre of the chart on pages 67–69. Mount your fabric in an embroidery frame if you wish.

2 Start stitching from the centre of the chart and fabric, using two strands of stranded cotton (floss) for full and three-quarter cross stitches and one strand for backstitches. Use one strand of metallic thread. Attach seed beads using a beading needle and matching thread (see page 91).

3 Decorate a tassel by threading eight seed beads on black thread and attaching to the tassel. Decorate three more tassels and attach them at the positions shown by white stars on the chart. For making your own tassels, see page 102.

4 Once stitching is complete and the tassels are in place, finish your picture by mounting in a suitable frame (see page 93).

Stitching the
Smaller Projects

The pagoda design can be used as a wonderful resource for lots of smaller projects – here and overleaf you will see some of the smaller motifs being used to decorate a bag, a bracelet and a notebook. The Oriental Inspiration panel overleaf suggests more ways that the designs could be used. For further inspiration see Making Up, beginning on page 93.

Dragonfly Bag

Stitch count 22h x 62w
Design size 4 x 11.2cm (1½ x 4½in)

This beautiful bag features the dragonfly from the pagoda chart. It was stitched over two threads of 28-count cream linen band but you could work over one block of 14-count Aida instead. I omitted the dark orange DMC 720 background stitches and only backstitched the dragonflies. I embellished the bag with a handle made of assorted beads and little bead drops at the corners. See page 99 for instructions on making up the bag.

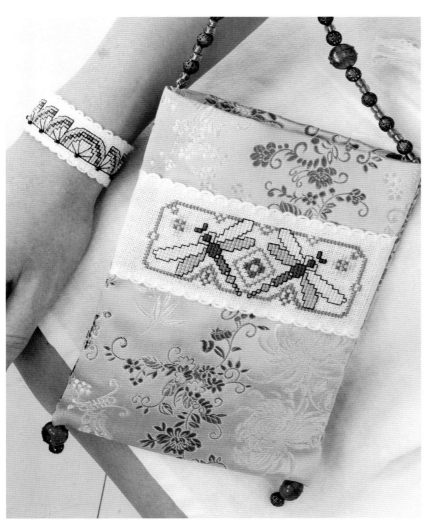

Fan Bracelet

Stitch count 8h x length required to fit wrist
Design size 1.3cm (½in) x length to fit wrist

A charming little bracelet worked on 2.5cm (1in) wide cream 14-count Aida band is quick to stitch and a sweet idea for a young girl. I have chosen the row of fans from the pagoda chart but the butterfly would also work for a wider band. See page 99 for making up the bracelet.

On the spring equinox
clouds wander about
the entrance of a
mountain temple.

Iida Dakotsu (1885–1962)

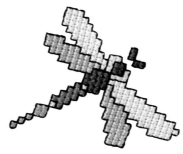

Blossom Notebook

Stitch count 59h x 16w
Design size 10.7 x 3cm (4¼ x 1¼in)

A decorated notebook is easy to achieve with a design stitched on 14-count Aida band or over two threads of a 28-count linen band. Measure the height of the book cover and double this for the length of band required. Stitch the motif from the pagoda chart and then fuse iron-on interfacing to the back of the embroidery to stabilize it. Use craft glue or double-sided tape to stick the band to the front of the book. Turn the surplus fabric to the inside of the book and glue or tape in place. Finally, cut a piece of card the same size as the inside cover and glue into position to cover the fabric edges.

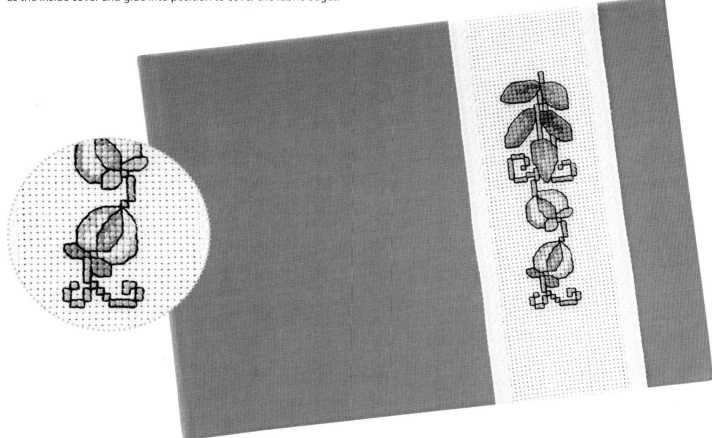

Oriental Inspiration

• In the Far East, bamboo is associated with writing as its stems are made into pens, so why not use the long bamboo motif to create an attractive bookmark on Aida or linen band?

• Glorious goldfish are bred in Japan, and those pictured in the flowing water in the pagoda design would make an elegant design for bathroom accessories, such as towel bands.

• Why not use the dragonflies, the swallows and the ornamental butterfly with grasses to decorate a series of greetings cards?

• The attractive fretwork patterns within the pagoda design would make lovely borders stitched on linen band to decorate fine bed linen.

Chasing dragonflies
today what place is it
he has strayed off to?

Kaga no Chiyo (1703–75)

Pagoda Splendour
DMC stranded cotton

Cross stitch (2 strands)

■	310	·	745	/	937	▨	3765	▨	3853
T	676	▨	747	▨	959	L	3766	O	3854
▬	720	/	807	—	3347	▨	3814	▨	3855
▨	729	■	920	▨	3348	+	3847		

Kreinik #4 Braid
▨ 202HL Aztec gold
(1 strand)

Backstitch (1 strand)
— 310

Mill Hill seed beads
● 02014 black

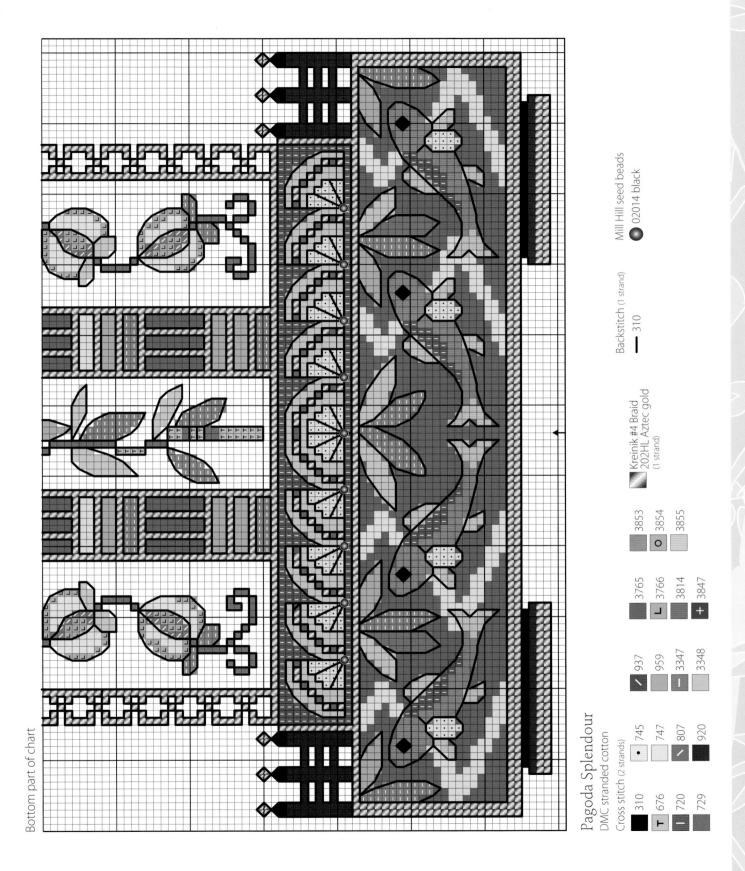

Bottom part of chart

Pagoda Splendour
DMC stranded cotton

Cross stitch (2 strands)

■	310	·	745	
T	676		747	
—	720	/	807	
—	729		920	

/	937		3765		3853
	959	L	3766	O	3854
—	3347		3814		3855
	3348	+	3847	

Kreinik #4 Braid
202HL Aztec gold
(1 strand)

Backstitch (1 strand)
— 310

Mill Hill seed beads
● 02014 black

Bamboo Linen

According to Japanese tradition, bamboo, the inspiration for this chapter, is one of the 'three friends of winter'; the other two being plum and pine. All three are considered to be good omens because in the cold season, when most plants are dormant, the bamboo and pine remain green, while the plum is the first to bloom after the cold winter. The Japanese believe that these three plants have great fortitude and uprightness in adverse conditions. Bamboo grows quickly to its full height, and this strength and upright growth are seen as desirable qualities in a young man. Such vigour indicates nobility, honesty and serious character.

The other motif used in the cutlery case design is a fan, which has played an important role in Asian life for many centuries (see also the Fan and Lantern chapter beginning on page 6). Carried by both men and women, there were different classes of fans, each reserved for a special occasion. The ribs of a folding fan were often made of bamboo, with painted paper pasted on to the ribs.

A cuckoo calls
and through the great
bamboo grove
I see the moon.
Matsuo Basho (1644–94)

A simple but elegant design of bamboo leaves is used for the table mat and coaster shown here. The cutlery case, made from an Aida band, is a simple way to store individual chopsticks or cutlery. The idea for this came from traditional 19th century Korean spoon cases, which were embroidered by the bride for her dowry or given as gifts, particularly at weddings. These were decorated with numerous longevity symbols, including cranes, pine trees, turtles and bamboo.

The three projects make a lovely table setting and would suit many different décors. They are all very easy to stitch and make up.

Stitching the
Bamboo Table Mat

This table mat, which could also become a napkin, has been worked on Aida fabric but you could use a 28-count linen if you prefer, working over two fabric threads.

Stitch count 142h x 33w
Design size 25.8 x 6cm (10¼ x 2½in)

You will need
- 46 x 40.5cm (18 x 16in) cream 14-count Aida
- Tapestry needle size 24
- DMC stranded cotton (floss) as listed in the chart key
- Matching sewing thread

1 Prepare for work, referring to page 89 if necessary. Mark the centre of the Aida fabric and centre of the chart on page 75. Mount your fabric in an embroidery frame if you wish.

2 Begin stitching from the centre of the fabric and chart and work outwards. Work cross stitches using two strands of stranded cotton (floss). Work backstitches using one strand.

3 Once stitching is complete, decide on the size of your mat or napkin and mark the outline with a line of machine stitching or backstitching in a matching thread. Cut the Aida 18 squares out from the design all round and then fray the fabric back to the line of stitching.

Stitching the
Bamboo Coaster

A set of coasters or small mats would be quick to stitch with this simple bamboo design. The edges of the Aida square are frayed as a pretty finishing touch.

Stitch count 42h x 40w
Design size 7.6 x 7.3cm (3 x 2¾in)

You will need
- 19 x 19cm (7½ x 7½in) cream 14-count Aida
- Tapestry needle size 24
- DMC stranded cotton (floss) as listed in the chart key
- Kreinik #4 Very Fine Braid, 028 citron
- Matching sewing thread

1 Prepare for work. Mark the centre of the Aida fabric and the centre of the chart on page 75.

2 Begin stitching from the centre of the fabric and chart. Work cross stitches using two strands of stranded cotton (floss) and one strand of Kreinik. Work backstitches in one strand.

3 To finish, cut the Aida 10 squares out from the design all round and then sew a line of machine stitching or backstitching in a matching thread all around, about five squares out from the design. Finish by fraying the edges back to the line of stitching.

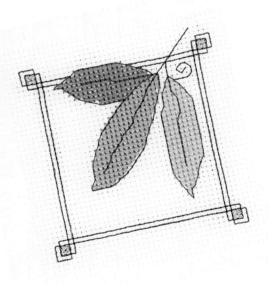

Stitching the Fan Cutlery Case

This attractive case could be used to hold chopsticks or other cutlery, or perhaps become a mobile phone case or even a glasses case.

Stitch counts
Flap with fan 35h x 46w
Main section 98h x 46w

Design sizes
Flap with fan 6.4 x 8.4cm (2½ x 3¼in)
Main section 18 x 8.4cm (7 x 3¼in)
Finished case size 26.5 x 10cm (10½ x 4in) approximately

You will need
- 54.6cm (21½in) long x 10cm (4in) wide cream 14-count Aida band
- Tapestry needle size 24
- DMC stranded cotton (floss) as listed in the chart key
- Kreinik #4 Very Fine Braid, 028 citron
- Tacking (basting) thread and matching sewing thread
- Three tassels and a few gold beads (optional)

1 Prepare for work, referring to page 89 if necessary. The diagram here shows the case dimensions and the stitching positions of the two motifs. Tack (baste) guidelines before you start, to show where the charts start and oversew the raw edges to prevent fraying. Mount your fabric in an embroidery frame if you wish.

2 Following the main section chart overleaf, begin by stitching 45 stitches from the start of the band and work down to the base of the embroidery. Work the cross stitches in stranded cotton (floss) in two strands, the Kreinik cross stitches in one strand and backstitches in one strand.

3 Turn the Aida band four squares from the bottom of the stitched design and fold the band towards the back. Count 142 squares along the back of the band and then turn the band forward to make a flap. Count two squares down from the fold and this is the position for the outer backstitch of the smaller design. Complete the fan design on the flap following the fan chart overleaf.

4 Once stitching is complete turn the ends of the Aida band under six rows and slipstitch in place. Fold the band in the correct position (see diagram). Remove tacking (basting) threads and machine or hand sew the side edges in a matching thread. Now make three tassels (see page 102), sew on a few gold beads for decoration and attach it to the top of the case.

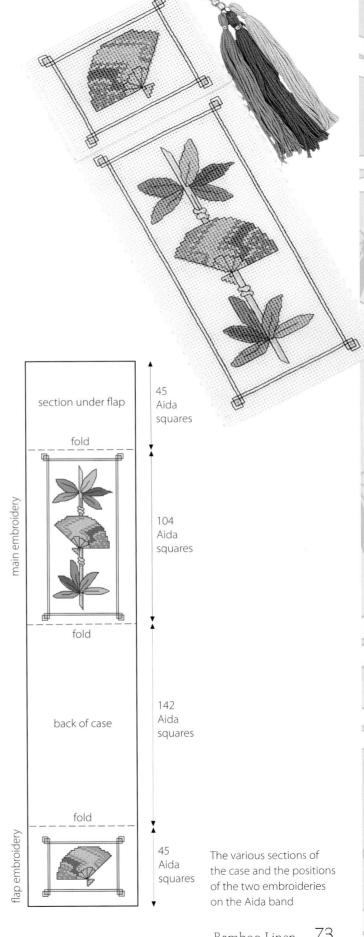

section under flap

fold

main embroidery

fold

back of case

fold

flap embroidery

45 Aida squares

104 Aida squares

142 Aida squares

45 Aida squares

The various sections of the case and the positions of the two embroideries on the Aida band

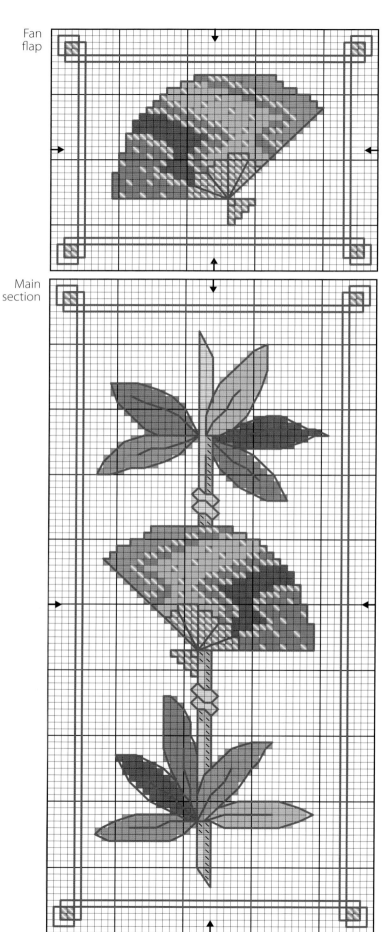

Fan
flap

Main
section

Fan Cutlery Case

DMC stranded cotton

Cross stitch (2 strands)

	598
	677
	987
	989
\	3046
	3810
	Kreinik #4 Braid 028 citron (1 strand)

Backstitch (1 strand)

— 3808

In my garden
a pretty bamboo clump
is stirring slightly.
What a subtle sound
of this evening breeze!
Ohtomo Yakamochi (718–785)

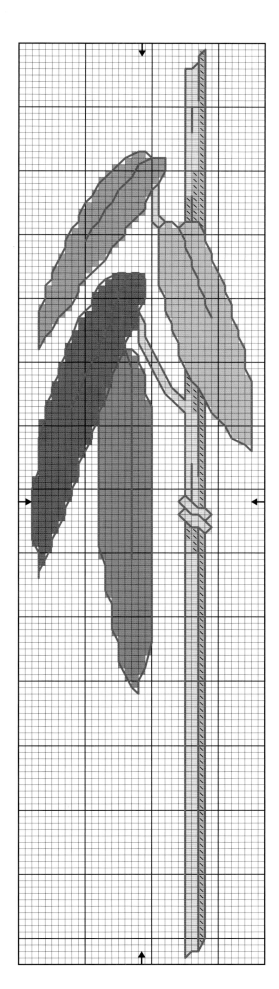

Bamboo Table Mat

DMC stranded cotton

Cross stitch (2 strands)

- 598
- 677
- 987
- 989
- 3046
- 3810

Backstitch (1 strand)

—— 3808

Bamboo Coaster

DMC stranded cotton

Cross stitch
(2 strands)

- 598
- 989
- 3810
- Kreinik #4 Braid
  028 citron (1 strand)

Backstitch
(1 strand)

—— 3808

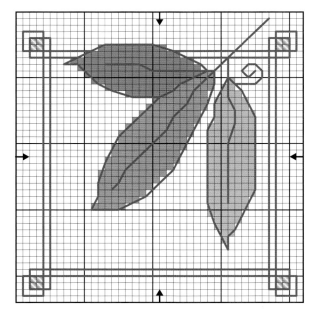

Oriental Beauty

This picture is a companion design to the Samurai Warrior on page 42 and depicts a sweetheart, serenely poised, patiently waiting for his return from battle, opening her beautiful decorated fan as an auspicious omen for the unfolding of the future.

Cherry blossom and peony flowers with butterflies were chosen as the decoration for the kimono, inspired by the elegance of exquisite prints found in the Japanese fabrics that make up the kimonos and *obi*, the sash. Cherry blossom, used as a hair decoration and as a simplified pattern on the sleeve, symbolizes their forthcoming wedding on the return of her beau. The peonies, 'the flower of 20 days', long venerated in China and Japan, bring hopes of prosperity to the couple. Flowing water, an ever-changing form that carries hope for a life of peace and harmony, links the combination of flowers and butterflies in a striking mixture of colour and pattern. The mauve flowers of the wisteria indicate a late spring scene, hanging in delicate clusters and cascading from the entwining vines. These beautiful flowers symbolize long life, prosperity and good fortune and family crests patterned with this flower are among the most traditional in Japan.

I have included a beautiful butterfly in the design as the Japanese regard the butterfly as an embodiment of the soul and the presence of a soul in this form is believed to bring luck and protection. You can work this lovely scene as a framed picture or take small motifs from the design to decorate other items – see overleaf for ideas.

In the autumn fields
mingled with the pampas grass
flowers are blooming
should my love too, spring forth
or shall we never meet?

From the love poems of the Kokinoshu
(a classic collection of Japanese verse)

Stitching the Oriental Beauty Picture

This beautiful Oriental lady is so elegant that she would grace almost any room.

Stitch count 211h x 82w
Design size 38.2 x 15cm (15 x 6in)

You will need
- 66 x 41cm (26 x 16in) antique white 14-count Aida
- Tapestry needle size 24 and a beading needle
- DMC stranded cotton (floss) as listed in the chart key
- Kreinik #4 Very Fine Braid, 002 gold
- Mill Hill antique glass beads, 03058 dark red
- Suitable picture frame

1 Prepare for work, referring to page 89 if necessary. Mark the centre of the fabric and centre of the chart. Mount your fabric in an embroidery frame if you wish.

2 Begin stitching from the centre of the fabric and centre of the chart and work outwards. Work the full and three-quarter cross stitches using two strands of stranded cotton (floss) and one strand for Kreinik cross stitches. Work the variously coloured backstitches using one strand of thread. (Note: black is shown in dark grey for clarity.) Work the French knots in the hair with one strand of gold metallic thread wound once round the needle, but use two strands of black stranded cotton wound once round the needle for the French knots on the butterfly.

3 Once all the stitching is complete, finish your picture by mounting in a suitable frame (see page 93 for advice).

Oriental Inspiration

- Other motifs from the Oriental Beauty chart could be stitched separately for gifts and cards. For example, you could work the wisteria on a length of Aida or linen band for a really pretty bookmark.

- The butterfly would make a lovely paperweight or a special greetings card, especially if you added a gleaming blending filament to the stranded cotton threads.

- The blossom in the girl's hair would be quick to stitch for a trinket pot lid, working French knots instead of beads – perfect as a gift to a friend.

DMC stranded cotton
Cross stitch (2 strands)

✕	729	○	150
╱	745	⌐	151
•	746	╱	155
╲	827		162
	905	▮	211
	962		225
┚	986	•	310
	3350	─	333
▮	3731	┖	505
	3746		535
╱	3799	┯	553
∨	3829		554
▨	Kreinik #4 Braid 002 gold (1 strand)		676
		─	703

Backstitch (1 strand)

	152
	310
	905
	3350
	Kreinik #4 Braid 002 gold

French knots
● 310 (2 strands)
◉ Kreinik #4 Braid 002 gold (1 strand)

Mill Hill antique glass beads
⬤ 03058 dark red

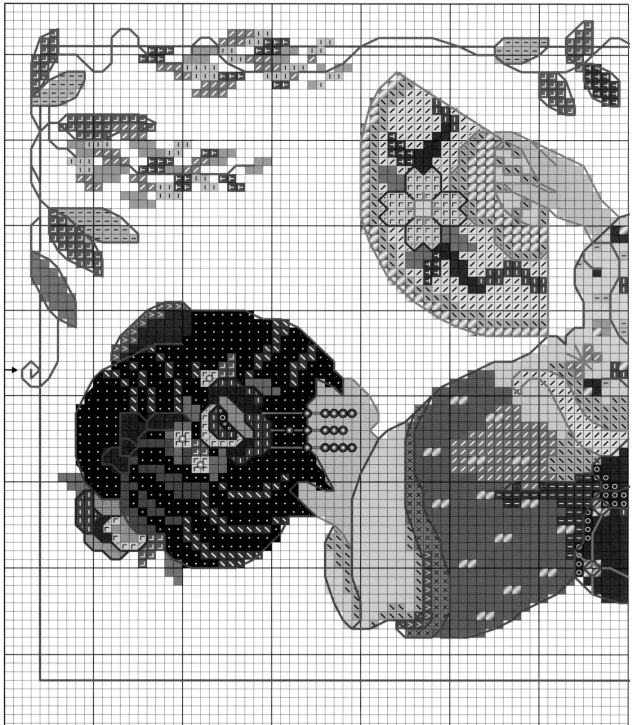

Top part of chart

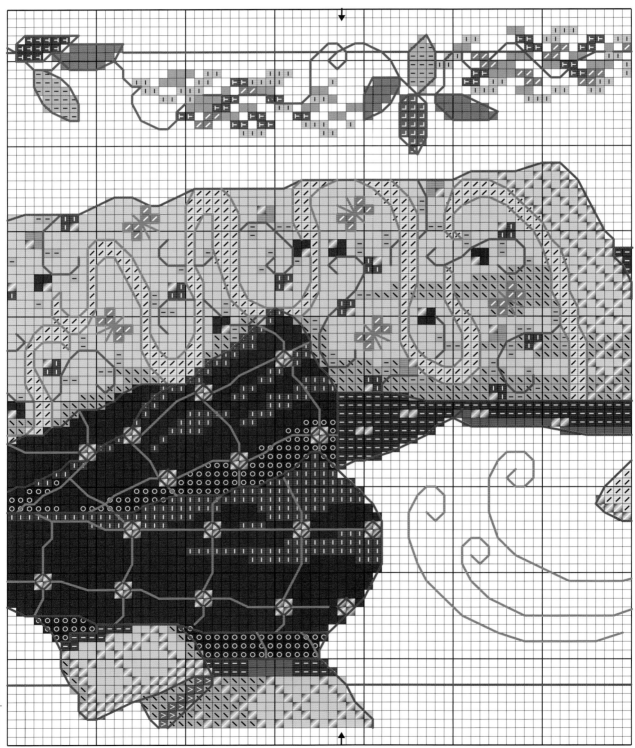

Oriental Beauty

DMC stranded cotton
Cross stitch (2 strands)

×	/	·	\					⊤			—			/	>	◹
729	745	746	827	905	962	986	3350	3731	3746	3799	3829	Kreinik #4 Braid 002 gold (1 strand)		

⊙	⌐	/							·	—	∟			⊤			—
150	151	155	162	211	225	310	333	505	535	553	554	676	703

Backstitch (1 strand)

152	310	905	3350	Kreinik #4 Braid 002 gold

French knots
● 310 (2 strands)
○ Kreinik #4 Braid 002 gold (1 strand)

Mill Hill antique glass beads
● 03058 dark red

Bottom part of chart

Blossom and Butterflies

An old Japanese word for spring is *sakuri-doki*, meaning cherry-blossom time, which is a reminder that life is brief and beauty fleeting, like the blossoms that fall while in their prime. This all-too-short period of time is the inspiration for this delicate bell pull design, showing a cascade of blossom interspersed with butterflies.

For as long as anyone has been able to record, cherry blossom has been the national flower of Japan. The Japanese love this flower for its beauty and delicacy, and value the lessons its short life brings – only when the petals begin to fall can you appreciate the fleeting beauty of this flower. It became an allegory for the short life of a feudal samurai, for he could be expected to sacrifice his life for his master at any time. A saying among the Japanese is 'the cherry is among flowers as the samurai is among men'. There are over 100 different varieties and they bloom each year on mainland Japan from March to May. Millions of people make pilgrimages to famous viewing sights every spring to enjoy this fleeting beauty.

Oh butterfly
what are you dreaming of
when you move your wings?
Chiyo-Ni (1701–75)

This very pretty bell pull with gorgeous butterflies scattered amongst the delicate blossom is simple to stitch and uses metallic thread with stranded cottons. Beads are added instead of French knots to bring a delicate decoration to the design. A matching card has been created using one of the butterfly motifs but there are many other ways you could use the design – see page 85 for ideas.

Stitching the
Butterflies Bell Pull

This lovely design is sure to draw admiring glances. Linen bands have attractive edges, which can be scalloped or pierced or coloured – look in your local craft store. If preferred you can use a 14-count Aida band instead, working over one block.

Stitch count 200h x 37w
Design size 36.3 x 6.7cm (14¼ x 2¾in)

You will need
- 56cm (22in) long x 12cm (4¾in) wide antique white 28-count Zweigart linen band
- Tapestry needle size 24 and a beading needle
- DMC stranded cotton (floss) as listed in the chart key
- Keinik #4 Very Fine Braid, 028 citron
- Mill Hill glass beads, 02008 sea breeze
- Mill Hill antique glass beads, 03058 Mardi gras red

1 Prepare for work, referring to page 89 if necessary. Mark the centre of the linen band and the centre of the chart overleaf. Use an embroidery frame if you wish.

2 Begin stitching from the centre of the band and work outwards over two linen threads. Work the full and three-quarter cross stitches using two strands of stranded cotton and one strand for the Kreinik cross stitches. Use one strand for the backstitches. Attach the beads where indicated on the chart, using a beading needle and matching thread (see page 91).

3 Once all the stitching is complete refer to page 98 for materials and instructions on making up the bell pull.

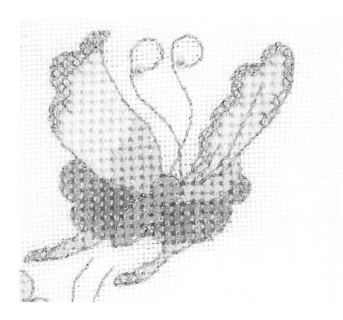

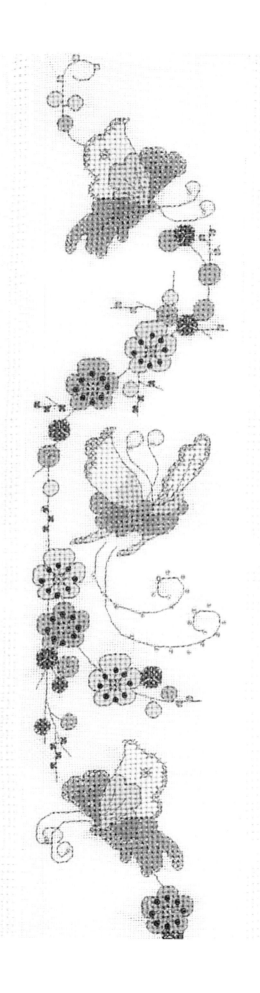

Butterfly Card

Stitch count 28h x 28w
Design size 5 x 5cm (2 x 2in)

This arched-aperture card in turquoise is a perfect choice for one of the butterflies from the bell pull. The motif is charted on page 87 and is stitched over one block of white 14-count Aida, using two strands of stranded cotton (floss) for cross stitch, one strand for the Kreinik thread cross stitches and one strand of thread for backstitch. See page 96 for mounting work in cards. It would be very easy to embellish this card – perhaps with a length of gold ribbon on the left side or with some twisted cord on the inside fold made from matching threads (see page 102 for making a twisted cord).

Oriental Inspiration

• Make a lovely mirror (see below) by stitching just the blossom, then turn the chart upside down and stitch it again, to create a space between the two designs. Mount the stitching on stiff card and stick a mirror tile in the centre.

• Create a pretty name plate for a door by stitching two of the butterflies and cross stitching or backstitching a name between them.

• Use individual motifs from the bell pull design to make a series of greetings cards or coasters.

• Embellish a T shirt or jeans by stitching a butterfly or small spray of blossom on 14-count Aida fabric. Back the embroidery with iron-on interfacing and then stitch on to the garment.

*Break open
a cherry tree
and there are no flowers,
but the spring breeze
brings forth myriad blossoms.*

Ikkyu Sojun (1394–1481)

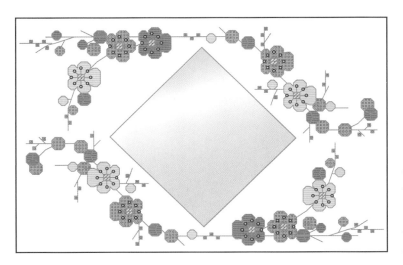

Follow the ideas in Oriental Inspirations to create lots of smaller projects or use your imagination to adapt the design completely, as in this mirror frame

Top part of chart

Butterflies Bell Pull

DMC stranded cotton
Cross stitch (2 strands)

	734
/	747
•	913
	958
L	959
	963
	964
O	3326
	3731
	Kreinik #4 Braid 028 citron (1 strand)

Backstitch (1 strand)

—— Kreinik #4 Braid
028 citron

Mill Hill glass beads

◯ 02008 sea breeze

◉ 03058 Mardi gras red

Bottom part of chart

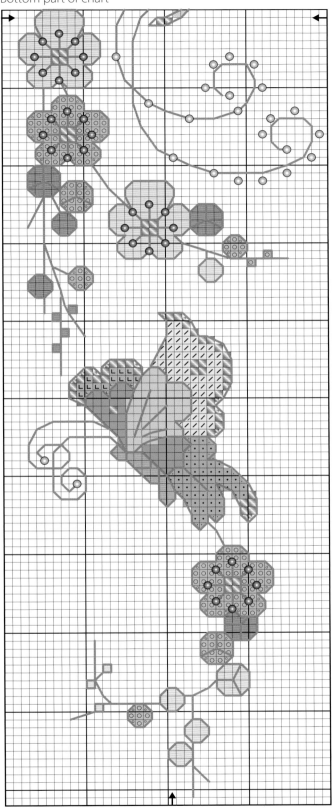

*From all directions
winds bring petals of cherry
into the grebe lake.*
Matsuo Basho (1644–94)

Materials, Techniques and Stitches

This section is useful to beginners as it describes the materials and equipment required and the basic techniques and stitches needed to work the projects. Refer to page 93 for making up methods and see Suppliers for useful addresses.

Materials

Very few materials are required for cross stitch embroidery, although some of the projects in this book have been given an additional sparkle and texture by the use of seed beads.

Fabrics
The designs have been worked predominantly on a blockweave fabric called Aida. If you change the gauge (count) of the material, that is the number of holes per inch, then the size of the finished work will alter accordingly. Some of the designs have been stitched on linen evenweave and in this case need to be worked over two fabric threads instead of one block.

Threads
The projects have been stitched with DMC stranded embroidery cotton (floss) but you could match the colours to other thread ranges – ask at your local needlework store about conversion charts. The six-stranded skeins of stranded cotton can easily be split into separate strands. The project instructions tell you how many strands to use. Some projects use one strand of a Kreinik metallic thread for added glitter.

Needles
Tapestry needles, available in different sizes, are used for cross stitch as they have a rounded point and do not snag fabric. A thinner, beading needle will be needed to attach seed beads.

Scissors
You will need two pairs of scissors: a pair of dressmaking shears for cutting fabric and a small pair of sharp-pointed embroidery scissors for cutting and trimming threads.

Embroidery Frames
It is a matter of personal preference as to whether you use an embroidery frame or hoop to keep your fabric taut while stitching. Generally speaking, working with a frame helps to keep the tension even and prevent distortion, while working without a frame is faster and less cumbersome. There are various types on the market – look in your local needlework store.

Techniques

Cross stitch embroidery requires few complicated techniques but your stitching will look its best if you follow the simple guidelines below – see also the Perfect Stitching tips on page 92.

Preparing the Fabric

Before starting work, check the design size given with each project and make sure that this is the size you require for your finished embroidery. Your fabric should be at least 5cm (2in) larger all the way round than the finished size of the stitching, to allow for making up. Before beginning to stitch, neaten the fabric edges either by hemming or zigzagging to help prevent fraying as you work.

Finding the Fabric Centre

Marking the centre of the fabric is important, regardless of which direction you work from, in order to stitch the design centrally on the fabric. To find the centre, fold the fabric in half horizontally and then vertically, then tack (baste) along the folds (or use tailor's chalk). The centre point is where the two lines of tacking (basting) meet. This point on the fabric should correspond to the centre point on the chart. Remove these lines on completion of the work.

Calculating Design Size

Each project gives the stitch count and finished design size but if you want to work the design on a different count fabric you will need to re-calculate the finished size. Divide the numbers of stitches in the design by the fabric count number, e.g. 140 x 140 ÷ 14-count = a design size of 10 x 10in (25.5 x 25.5cm). Working on evenweave usually means working over two threads, so divide the fabric count by two before you start calculating.

Starting and Finishing Stitching

Avoid using knots when starting and finishing as this will make your work lumpy when mounted. Instead, bring the needle up at the start of the first stitch, leaving a 'tail' of about 2.5cm (1in) at the back. Secure the tail by working the first few stitches over it. Start new threads by first passing the needle through several stitches on the back of the work.

To finish off thread, pass the needle through some nearby stitches on the wrong side of the work, then cut the thread off, close to the fabric.

Washing and Pressing

If you need to wash your finished embroidery, first make sure the stranded cottons are colourfast by washing them in tepid water and mild soap. Rinse well and lay out flat to dry completely before stitching. Wash completed embroideries in the same way. Iron on a medium setting, covering the ironing board with a thick layer of towelling. Place stitching right side down and press gently. Take care if beads or metallic threads have been used.

Using Charts and Keys

The charts in this book are easy to work from. Each square on the chart represents one stitch. Each coloured square, or coloured square with a symbol, represents a thread colour, with the code number given in the chart key (see the example here). A few of the designs use fractional stitches (three-quarter stitches) to give more definition to the design, shown on charts as triangles. Solid coloured lines show where backstitches or long stitches are to be worked. French knots are shown by coloured circles. Larger coloured circles indicate beads. Each complete chart has arrows at the side to show the centre point, which you could mark with a pen. Where the charts have been split over several pages, the key is repeated. For your own use, you could colour photocopy and enlarge charts, taping the parts together.

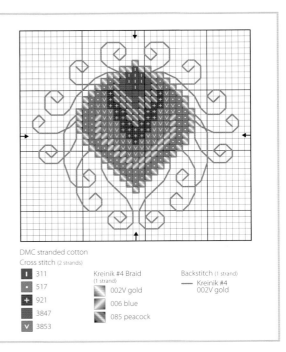

DMC stranded cotton
Cross stitch (2 strands)

▮ 311	**Kreinik #4 Braid** (1 strand)	**Backstitch** (1 strand)
● 517	◨ 002V gold	— Kreinik #4 002V gold
✚ 921	◨ 006 blue	
▨ 3847	◨ 085 peacock	
V 3853		

The Stitches

The stitches used for the projects in this book are all very easy to work – simply follow the advice and diagrams here.

Backstitch

Backstitches are used to give definition to parts of a design and to outline areas. Many of the charts used different coloured backstitches and the codes are given in the chart key. Follow Fig 1, bringing the needle up at 1 and down at 2. Then bring the needle up again at 3, down at 4 and so on.

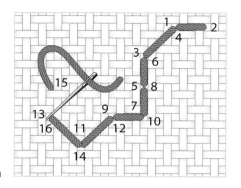

Fig 1 Working backstitch

Cross Stitch

A cross stitch can be worked singly over one block of Aida (Fig 2a) or over two threads of linen or evenweave fabric (Fig 2b). You can also work cross stitch in two journeys, working a number of half stitches in a line and completing the stitches on the return journey (Fig 2c).

To make a cross stitch over one block of Aida, bring the needle up through the fabric at the bottom left side of the stitch (number 1 on Fig 2a) and cross diagonally to the top right corner (2). Push the needle through the hole and bring up through the bottom right corner (3), crossing the fabric diagonally to the top left corner to finish the stitch (4). To work the next stitch, come up through the bottom right corner of the first stitch (at 3) and repeat the sequence above.

To work a line of cross stitches, stitch the first part of the stitch as above and repeat these half cross stitches along the row. Complete the crosses on the way back. Note: for neat work, always finish the cross stitch with the top stitches lying in the same diagonal direction.

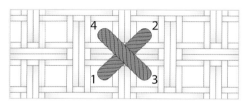

Fig 2a Working a single cross stitch on Aida

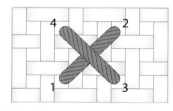

Fig 2b Working cross stitch on linen or evenweave fabric

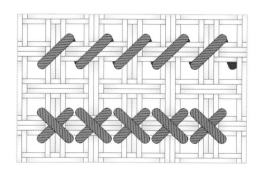

Fig 2c Working cross stitch in two journeys

French Knot

French knots have been used as highlights and details in some of the designs, in various colours. To work, follow Fig 3, bringing the needle and thread up through the fabric at the exact place where the knot is to be positioned. Wrap the thread once or twice around the needle (according to the project instructions), holding the thread firmly close to the needle, then twist the needle back through the fabric as close as possible to where it first emerged. Holding the knot down carefully, pull the thread through to the back leaving the knot on the surface, securing it with one small stitch on the back.

Fig 3 Working a French knot

Long Stitch

This is a very easy stitch. Work a long, straight stitch (Fig 4) starting and finishing at the points shown on the chart.

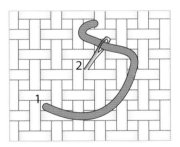

Fig 4 Working a long stitch

Three-quarter Cross Stitch

Three-quarter cross stitches give more detail to a design and can create the illusion of curves. They are shown by a triangle within a square on the charts (examples shown in Fig 5). Working three-quarter cross stitches is easier on evenweave fabric than Aida (see Fig 5). To work on Aida, make a quarter stitch from the corner into the centre of the Aida square, piercing the fabric, and then work a half stitch across the other diagonal.

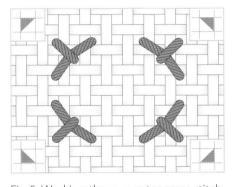

Fig 5 Working three-quarter cross stitch

Attaching Beads

Beads can bring sparkle and texture to your cross stitch embroidery and are a lovely addition to many of the designs in this book. Attach seed beads using ordinary sewing thread that matches the fabric colour and a beading needle or very fine 'sharp' needle and a half cross stitch (Fig 6).

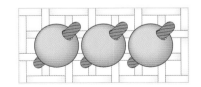

Fig 6 Attaching beads

Perfect Stitching

Counted cross stitch is one of the easiest forms of counted embroidery. Following these useful pointers when stitching the designs in this book will help you to produce neat and excellent work.

- Before starting, check the design size given with each project and make sure that this is the size you require for your finished embroidery.

- The fabric you are stitching on should be at least 5cm (2in) larger all round than the finished size of the stitching, to allow for making up.

- Organize your threads before you start a project as this will help to avoid confusion later. Put the threads required for a particular project on an organizer (available from craft shops) and always include the manufacturer's name and the shade number. You can easily make your own thread organizer by using a hole punch to punch holes along one side of a piece of thick card.

- When you have cut the length of stranded cotton (floss) you need, usually about 46cm (18in), separate out all the strands before taking the number you need, realigning them and threading your needle.

- When stitching with metallic threads, work with shorter lengths, about 30cm (12in) to avoid tangling and excessive wear on the thread.

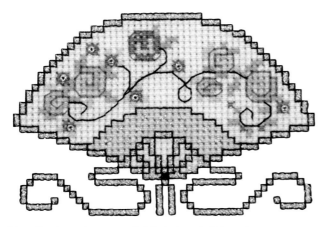

Metallic threads are available in irresistible colours

- If using a frame, try to avoid using a hoop as it can stretch the fabric and leave a mark that may be difficult to remove. If you do use a hoop, avoid placing it over worked stitches and remove it from the fabric at the end of a stitching session.

- Plan your route carefully around the chart, counting over short distances where possible to avoid making counting mistakes. Check your position frequently.

- Whenever possible, work your cross stitch in two directions in a sewing movement – half cross stitch in one direction and then cover those original stitches with the second row. This forms vertical lines on the back and gives somewhere to finish off raw ends tidily.

- For neat cross stitching, work the top stitches so they all face in the same direction.

- Avoid bringing the needle up through occupied holes from the back, where there is already a stitch, as you may snag and spoil the existing stitch. Insert the needle from the front wherever possible.

- If your thread begins to twist, turn the work upside down and let the needle spin, which will unwind the thread.

- Take care when turning your work or you may inadvertently change the direction of the top stitch on your cross stitch and spoil the neat look of your work.

- If adding a backstitch outline, always add it after the cross stitch has been completed to prevent the solid line of the backstitch being broken.

Small motifs come alive with delicate backstitching, which is invaluable not only for making details stand out clearly with outlining but also to create attractive shapes

Making Up

The embroideries in this book have been made up in many varied ways, including pictures, cards, cushions, box tops, albums and table linen. The methods used are described here, but the designs are very versatile so why not experiment with other ways? Metric and imperial measurements have been provided but remember to use one or the other as they are not exactly interchangeable.

Framing as a Picture

There are many stunning pictures in the book and how an embroidery is mounted and framed can make a great deal of difference to the finished look. It is advisable to take your work to a professional framer for a wide choice of mounts and frames, especially where multi-apertures are needed, such as the Geisha Triptych from page 19, or the Oriental Blooms flower embroideries, shown on page 49.

You will need

- Piece of plywood or heavyweight card slightly smaller than the frame
- Suitable picture frame (aperture size to fit embroidery)
- Mount, if one is being used
- Adhesive tape or a staple gun

1 Iron your embroidery, taking care if any beads or metallic threads have been used, and trim the edges if necessary, then centre the embroidery on to the piece of plywood or thick card.

2 Fold the edges of the embroidery to the back of the plywood or card and use adhesive tape or a staple gun to fix it in place all around.

3 If using a mount place it over the embroidery from the front, ensuring the design is centred in the mount. Fix lightly in place at the sides.

4 Insert the mounted embroidery into the frame and secure the back of the frame with more adhesive tape or staples.

Attaching Embroidery to a Background Fabric

The Fan and Lantern picture (page 7) and the Oriental Landscape picture (page 30) are finished by fusing the embroidery to a fusible web such as Vilene, then framing. Many of the other designs would be suited to this way of framing. For example, the flower designs from the Oriental Blooms chapter (pages 48–55) would look attractive with a fabric background. Experiment to see what different effects can be achieved.

You will need
• Background fabric
• Iron-on interfacing, such as Vilene
• Decorative braid, tassel and buttons
• Suitable picture frame

1 When the embroidery is finished, use the weave of the fabric as a guide to trim within ten rows of the design (or a border to a width you desire). Press the stitched piece and iron the interfacing on the back of the embroidery to stabilize it. Fold over the edges by eight rows – to leave two rows showing around the design (or more if you prefer). Press these folds into place.

2 Find the centre of the background fabric and the centre of the embroidery, and pin or tack (baste) guidelines for the position of the embroidery (see diagram here for positioning the Oriental Landscape designs). Place the embroidery on the fabric and slipstitch in place with matching thread.

3 Add a length of decorative cord all around the edge of each embroidery, starting at bottom centre and slipstitching it into place, or gluing it with permanent fabric glue.

4 To finish off, stitch or glue on a decorative bead or button where the cord ends meet. For the Fan and Lantern picture I used black decorative cord and added a black tassel (see page 102 for making your own tassels).

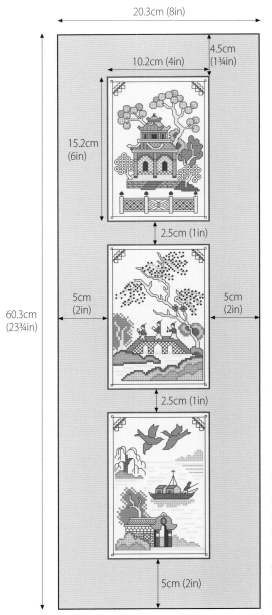

20.3cm (8in)

4.5cm (1¾in)

10.2cm (4in)

15.2cm (6in)

2.5cm (1in)

5cm (2in)   5cm (2in)

60.3cm (23¾in)

2.5cm (1in)

5cm (2in)

Positions of the three embroideries on the background fabric for the Oriental Landscape picture. Alternatively, you could have a mount cut using these measurements.

Mounting Work into Cards

Many of the designs or parts of larger designs can be stitched and made up into lovely greetings cards. There are many styles of card mounts available today. Some are simple single-fold cards, while others are pre-folded with three sections, the middle one having a window or aperture for your embroidery.

Mounting Work on a Single-Fold Card

Craft stores are full of lovely single-fold cards in all shapes, sizes and colours, but it is also very easy to make your own cards using some of the fabulous range of cardstock available today.

1 To mount embroidery on a single-fold card, start by backing your embroidery with iron-on interfacing to stabilize the edges and prevent fraying. Now trim your embroidery to the size required leaving a narrow border all round.

2 Use double-sided tape or a thin layer of fabric glue to attach the embroidery to the front of your card. Be careful that no glue oozes out at the sides of the embroidery.

If you want a fringe around your embroidery, then cut a piece of interfacing slightly smaller than the embroidery and fuse it to the centre of the work, leaving a border all round. When the stitching has been glued or stuck to the front of your card you can then use a needle to tease away the loose outer threads to create a fringe.

For a personal touch you could add ribbons, braids, bows, buttons or other pretty embellishments to decorate your card, such as the ribbon and coin I used on the wedding card above.

Mounting Work in a Double-Fold Card

Double-fold cards are designed with three flaps: the middle flap has a window or aperture cut to house the embroidery, with a right-hand flap that folds over to hide the back of the embroidery. There is a huge range available from various manufacturers (see Suppliers for some addresses) or you could make you own following the instructions below.

1 To mount embroidery in a ready-made double-fold card, position the embroidery in the window space. The fabric should be slightly larger than the window, with the design itself fitting neatly into the window. Trim excess fabric from the embroidery, leaving it about 2.5cm (1in) bigger than the window all round.

2 Working from the inside of the card, place strips of double-sided adhesive tape around the window, close to the edges

(some cards already have this in place). Now peel off the backing tape and press the embroidery into position on the sticky tape.

3 Place more double-sided tape all around the edges of the centre portion of the card. Peel the backing from the tape and fold the right-hand flap of the card over and press into place to cover the back of the embroidery.

Making a Double-Fold Card

You can make your own double-fold cards quite easily and this will allow you to choose the right card colour to match your embroidery. The instructions below are for a small card but you can easily change the dimensions to suit your embroidery by working with a larger piece of cardstock. Choose a weight of card thick enough to support your stitching – between 160–240gsm.

You will need
- Thick cardstock in a colour of your choice
- Cutting mat
- Craft knife and metal ruler
- Embossing tool and bone folder (optional)

1 Choose a card colour to complement your embroidery and cut a piece 30 x 12cm (12 x 4¾in) as shown in the diagram below (or to the size of your choice). On the wrong side of the card, use a pencil to draw two lines dividing it into three sections of 10cm (4in). Score gently along each line with the back of a craft knife or with an embossing tool to make folding easier. Don't cut through the card.

2 In the centre section, mark an aperture slightly bigger than the finished size of the design, leaving a border of about 2.5cm (1in) at the top and bottom and about 1.25cm (½in) at the sides. Place the card on a cutting mat and cut out the aperture with a sharp craft knife and metal ruler, cutting into the corners carefully and neatly.

3 Trim the left edge of the first section by about 2mm (⅛in) so that it lies flat when folded over to the inside of the card. This will cover the back of the stitching. Fold the left and then the right section on the scored lines – a bone folder with help you to create a nice, sharp fold. The card is now ready for you to mount your embroidery.

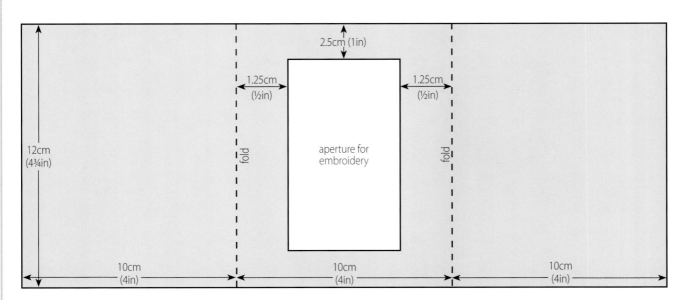

Making a double-fold aperture card

Making a Bell Pull

I used a linen band to make the Blossom and Butterflies bell pull (see page 84) but an Aida fabric band will work as well. Or you could use a piece of linen or Aida and hem the sides.

You will need
- Iron-on interfacing, same size as finished embroidery
- Length of dowelling slightly longer than the band width
- Small pot of paint to tone with embroidery
- Permanent fabric glue
- Three tassels (bought or home made)
- 1m (1yd) of narrow ribbon in a matching colour

1 Once the design is stitched, trim it to size allowing enough fabric to go over the dowelling rod. Iron the interfacing on to the back of the band to stabilize the stitches and make the fabric a little firmer. Fold the bottom of the band to form a point and then slipstitch in place.

2 Using matching sewing thread, sew the tassels to the base, one at each corner and one at the point. To make your own tassels, see page 102.

3 Paint the dowelling and allow it to dry thoroughly. A little 'match' pot of emulsion paint works well and dries quite quickly. Fold the top of the band over the dowelling rod and sew it to the back of the band.

4 Cut the length of ribbon in two, attaching one length to each side of the rod with fabric glue. Tie the ribbons in a bow and use to hang the bell pull.

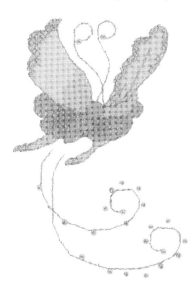

Making a Bag

The flower designs (page 48) and the bands from Pagoda Splendour (page 63) are ideal for bags. You could use motifs from the Fan and Lantern design (page 7) and an individual picture from the Oriental Landscapes chapter (pages 30–35).

You will need

- Two rectangles of background fabric the size you require, plus 1.25cm (½in) all round for turnings for the bag
- Two rectangles of lining fabric the same size
- Decorative satin cord to tone with fabric, to fit around the embroidery
- Tassels and beads as required
- Cord for a handle or a bead handle
- Stranded cotton (floss) to match cord

1 Attach the embroidery or Aida band to the front piece of the bag fabric following steps 1 and 2 on page 94 – as a guide allow an equal border of fabric all round.

2 If making the poppy bag on page 50, stitch the cord round the embroidery starting at the centre bottom, tacking (basting) the ends together with a few small stitches. Attach a button or bead at the centre bottom with matching thread.

3 Place the lining fabric pieces right sides together and, with a 1.25cm (½in) seam allowance, machine along two long sides and one short side. Repeat with the bag fabric pieces.

4 Place the lining bag inside the embroidered bag, wrong sides together. Turn top raw edges inside. Cut cord for the handle (or make a bead handle) and place 2.5cm (1in) of cord along the seams between the two layers, sewing in place with matching thread. Now slipstitch the turnings with matching thread. Add tassels and beads for further decoration as desired.

Making a Bracelet

Many of the designs in the book have motifs that can be used for small gifts, such as this little bracelet. Worked on Aida band, the bracelet is very quick to make up.

You will need

- Iron-on interfacing
- Bracelet fastening
- Beads for decoration as required
- Matching sewing thread

1 Iron your finished embroidery and turn under the ends and catch with a few stitches.

2 Cut a strip of iron-on interfacing to the size of the bracelet and fuse it to the wrong side.

3 Attach the bracelet fastening to the Aida band with matching sewing thread.

4 Make an additional bead and tassel decoration (see page 64) if required and sew this to the bracelet.

Mounting Work in Box Lids

Wood workboxes are perfect for storing needlecraft threads and accessories. Make sure the aperture on your chosen box lid is the correct size for your embroidery. Most manufacturer's include mounting instructions with the box, so follow these or the description below.

You will need
- Box with lid suitable for embroidery
- Thick card the size of the box lid
- Wadding (batting) (optional)
- Double-sided adhesive tape
- Decorative cord or braid
- Permanent fabric glue

1 Once stitching is complete cut thick card slightly smaller than the size of the box lid aperture.

2 Trim the embroidery, allowing enough fabric to wrap to the back of the thick card. For a raised effect, add layers of wadding (batting) on the card and place the embroidery on top of these layers. Alternatively, just place the embroidery centrally on the card and fold the surplus fabric to the back of the card. Secure the corners with double-sided adhesive tape

and then fold the edges of the fabric neatly and secure with more tape.

3 Place the embroidery into the box lid aperture. Slip the piece of wood provided with the box in behind, clipping it into place in the opening.

4 Finish by adding decorative cord around the embroidery, securing in place with fabric glue.

Making a Cushion

The Mandarin Ducks design (page 38) and the Crane Ring Cushion design (page 59) have been made into cushions and the following instructions are for making a pillow or cushion in any size you want. Smaller embroideries can be attached to backing fabric, as described on the previous page, and then made up into a cushion.

You will need
- Cushion pad or polyester stuffing
- Backing fabric
- Matching sewing thread
- Tassels and cord (optional)
- Decorative button (optional)

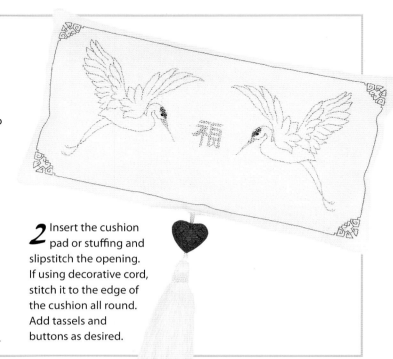

1 Cut the backing fabric to the same size as the trimmed embroidery, place right sides together and pin. Use matching sewing thread to stitch a 1.25cm (½in) seam all round, leaving an opening at the bottom for turning through.

2 Insert the cushion pad or stuffing and slipstitch the opening. If using decorative cord, stitch it to the edge of the cushion all round. Add tassels and buttons as desired.

Making Up into an Album

Linen and Aida bands are a great way to display designs and are very quick to mount on to the front of a purchased album, diary or notebook as you can see by this Wedding Album design, shown on page 58.

You will need
- A ready-made album or notebook
- Iron-on interfacing
- Double-sided adhesive tape

1 Take your finished embroidery and trim the stitched band to the size you require for your album or book.

2 Iron the interfacing on to the back of your work to stiffen the fabric and stabilize the stitches.

3 Place the band on the album or book and turn the ends under the front cover. Slipstitch in place, or secure with double-sided adhesive tape.

Making a Purse

The orchid design from page 53 was made up into a lovely little purse but many other designs from the book would work well too.

You will need
- Background fabric to the size required
- Lining material to the size required
- Zip to the size required
- Decorative satin cord tone with fabric, to fit around the embroidery
- Tassel and buttons as required

1 Cut two pieces of background fabric to the size required – as a guide, allow 5cm (2in) larger than the design, plus 1.25cm (½in) for turnings. When using Aida and linen bands adapt the measurements to suit. Cut two pieces of lining fabric the same size as the background fabric.

2 Position the embroidery on the front panel. Allow an equal border of fabric all round and use matching sewing thread to attach the embroidery to the centre of the background fabric (or attach as described on page 94).

3 Stitch the cord around the embroidery starting at the centre bottom, tacking (basting) the ends together with a few small stitches. Attach a button or bead at the centre bottom using matching stranded cotton (floss).

4 Fold the top of the fabric under 1.25cm (½in) on both pieces of background fabric. Place the folded edge next to the teeth of the zip with the right sides up. Tack (baste) in place and then stitch by machine. Remove the tacking and open the zip. Fold the fabric right side together and machine along the other three sides, using a 1.25cm (½in) seam allowance. Turn the purse to the right side.

5 Place the lining fabric pieces right sides together and machine along three sides allowing a 1.25cm (½in) seam allowance. Turn to the right side.

6 Place the lining bag inside the purse wrong sides together and turn the raw edges of the lining under and slipstitch in place to the background fabric. Close the zip and add a bead and tassel decoration as desired. See page 102 for making your own tassels.

Making a Tassel

A tassel makes a nice finishing touch, for example on the corners of a cushion or sachet or at the end of a bookmark or bell pull. Making your own allows you to match the colours to your project.

1 To make a simple tassel, cut a rectangular piece of stiff card, about 1.5cm (½in) longer than the desired size of the tassel.

2 Choose a thread colour or colours to match your project and wrap the thread around the card to the desired thickness.

3 Slip a length of thread through the wound threads and then slide all the threads off the card. Tie the single thread in a knot.

4 Bind the top third of the tassel with another length of thread and then trim all the tassel ends to the same length.

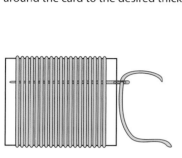

Ready-made tassels are often quite ornate but making your own, like this one from the cutlery case on page 73, allows you to select just the right colours

Making a Twisted Cord

A twisted cord can be used in various ways – to create a decorative edging to your stitching or a cushion or be placed in the fold of a card for a luxurious look or as a tie for gift tags. There are many decorative braids available but it is easy to make your own cord. Choose shades that match or tone with the embroidery for a co-ordinated look or pick a contrasting colour to act as a highlight. Experiment with metallic or other specialist threads for a sumptuous effect.

1 To make a single-colour cord, choose a shade from your embroidery design and cut a length of stranded cotton (floss) about three times longer than the finished cord.

2 Fold the thread in half and holding the two ends in one hand, pass the loop over the forefinger of your other hand or over a pencil. Now rotate your finger until the thread begins to twist and resemble a cord.

3 Continue twisting, holding the ends securely. Eventually the twisted thread will spring back on itself and you will have a silky smooth cord. Knot the loose ends securely, leaving enough thread to tease out into a tassel if desired.

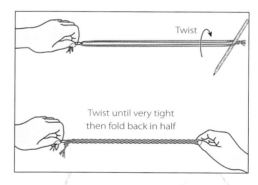

Twist

Twist until very tight then fold back in half

Making a length of twisted cord from embroidery threads

Suppliers

Beadworks (UK)
21a Tower Street, Covent Garden, London
WC2H 9NS, UK
Tel: 0208 553 3240
Email: customerservice@beadworks.co.uk
www.beadwork.co.uk
For beads and charms

Beadworks (USA)
167 Newberry Street, Boston
MA 02116, USA
Tel: 617 247 7227
www.boston@beadwork.com
For beads and charms

The Button Lady
16 Hollyfields South, Sutton Coldfield,
West Midlands, B76 1NX, UK
Tel: 01213 293 234
For buttons and charms

Coats Craft UK
PO Box 22, Lingfield Estate, McMullen
Road, Darlington, County Durham,
DL1 1YQ, UK
Tel: 01325 3654579 (for a list of stockists)
*For embroidery supplies and threads and
Kreinik metallic threads*

DMC Creative World
Pullman Road, Wigston, Leicestershire,
LE18 2DY, UK
Tel: 0116 281 1040
Fax: 0116 281 3592
www.dmc/cw.com
For embroidery supplies and threads

Dove of the East
Email: info@doveoftheeast.com
www.doveoftheeast.com
For charms

Framecraft Miniatures Ltd
Isis House, Linden Road, Brownhills,
West Midlands, WS8 7BW, UK
Tel: 01543 360 842
Fax: 01543 453 154
Email: sales@framecraft.com
www.framecraft.com
*For ready-made items with cross stitch
inserts, including bowls, trinket pots,
compact mirrors and pincushions*

Heritage Stitchcraft
Redbrook Lane, Brereton, Rugeley,
Staffordshire WS15 1QU, UK
Tel: +44 (0) 1889 575256
Email: enquiries@heritagestitchcraft.com
www.heritagestitchcraft.com
*For cross stitch fabrics including Zweigart,
bands, table linen and embroidery supplies*

Kreinik Manufacturing Company Inc
3106 Timanus Lane, Suite 101, Baltimore,
MD 21244, USA
Tel: 1800 537 2166
Email: kreinik@kreinik.com
www.kreinik.com
*For a wide range of metallic threads,
blending filaments and cords*

**Mill Hill, a division of Wichelt
Imports Inc.**
N162 Hwy 35, Stoddard
WI 54658, USA
Tel: 608 788 4600
Fax: 608 788 6040
Email: millhill@millhill.com
www. millhill.com
*For Mill Hill beads and a US source for
Framecraft products*

Stitch Direct
Well Oast, Brenley Lane, Brenley,
Faversham, Kent, ME13 9LY, UK
Tel: 01227 750 215
Fax: 01227 750 813
www.stitchdirect.com
For the table-top workbox

The Viking Loom
22 High Petergate, York, YO1 7EH, UK
Tel: 01904 765 599
www.vikingloom.co.uk
For bell pulls and linen bands

Zweigart/Joan Toggit Ltd
262 Old New Brunswick Road, Suite E,
Piscataway, NJ 08854 0 3756, USA
Tel: 732 562 8888
Email: info@zweigart.com
www.zweigart.com
*For cross stitch fabrics, bands and
table linens*

About the Author

Lesley Teare

Lesley trained as a textile designer, with a degree in printed and woven textiles. For some years she has been one of DMC's leading designers and her designs have also featured in many of the cross stitch magazines. Lesley has contributed to six other books for David & Charles: *Cross Stitch Greetings Cards, Cross Stitch Alphabets, Cross Stitch Angels, Cross Stitch Fairies, Magical Cross Stitch* and *Quick to Stitch Cross Stitch Cards*. Her book *101 Weekend Cross Stitch Gifts* was followed by *Travel the World in Cross Stitch*. Lesley lives in Hitcham, Suffolk.

Acknowledgments

Yet another mammoth undertaking for Tina Godwin who as usual has brought her skills and talent to stitching all the designs in this book. It is really good to have someone so dedicated so that we get the best from my designs, especially when there are times that are occasionally fraught with deadlines and artist blocks, and Tina stays calm and focused. My thanks and love.

Katherine Keatling at Heritage Stitchcraft who has supplied all the wonderful fabrics and who worked closely with Tina to get the best possible results for all the projects. Rebecca Jackson from DMC who supplied the stranded cottons and Susan Spears at Coats Craft for the beautiful Kreinik threads. Michael Oxley for making such a wonderful job again with all the framing and Maureen Ashford at Framecraft for providing all the lovely products for the small needlework projects.

My thanks go to all the people at David & Charles whose efforts have made this book possible. Special appreciations to Cheryl Brown, whose enthusiasm and skills have once again guided me through the writing and designing of this book, Pru Rogers for her artistic flair in putting the book design together and Jenny Proverbs and Bethany Dymond in editing the book so well. Finally, Lin Clements who as project editor made everything go so smoothly as well as working on all the charts for this book. Very many thanks Lin.

Index